Joy &
Peace

The following Oswald Chambers books are available from Discovery House Publishers:

Biblical Ethics

Biblical Psychology

Christian Disciplines

Complete Works of Oswald Chambers

Conformed to His Image
   / The Servant as His Lord

Faith: A Holy Walk

Hope: A Holy Promise

If You Will Ask

Joy & Peace: A Holy Condition

Love: A Holy Command

The Love of God

My Utmost for His Highest

Our Brilliant Heritage / If You Will Be Perfect
   / Disciples Indeed

Our Ultimate Refuge

Prayer: A Holy Occupation

So Send I You / Workmen of God

Studies in the Sermon on the Mount

Joy &
Peace
A Holy
Condition

Oswald Chambers

Compiled and Edited by
JULIE ACKERMAN LINK

DISCOVERY HOUSE
PUBLISHERS

Joy & Peace: A Holy Condition
© 2011 by Oswald Chambers Publications Association
Limited. All rights reserved.

Discovery House Publishers is affiliated with RBC
Ministries, Grand Rapids, Michigan.

Requests for permission to quote from this book
should be directed to: Permissions Department,
Discovery House Publishers, P.O. 3566,
Grand Rapids, MI, 49501, or contact us by e-mail
at permissionsdept@dhp.org

All Scripture quotations, unless otherwise indicated,
are from the New King James Version. Copyright ©
1979, 1980, 1982 by Thomas Nelson, Inc., Publishers.

Questions by Julie Ackerman Link

ISBN: 978-1-57293-455-9

Printed in the United States of America
12 13 14 15 16 17 / 10 9 8 7 6 5 4 3

Contents

Introduction

Joy and peace. Peace and Joy. The two are such close friends that we seldom find them alone. They show up together in greetings, in salutations, and in prayers. They are nearly inseparable during the Christmas season. And no wonder. Are any gifts more desirable than joy and peace? They are two of the most needed and valued states of being. They represent the end of longing and the satisfaction of desire.

Few things bring greater joy than a peaceful resolution to a conflict. If you are estranged from a loved one, will any gift from that person, no matter how expensive, bring as much joy as reconciliation? Surely not. If you have a wayward son or daughter, nothing brings more joy than a reunion, nothing is more welcome than peace restored.

Joy and peace are companions. We can't entertain them separately.

The lack of joy and peace indicate dissatisfaction. And all dissatisfaction ultimately goes back to God; it's an expression of our disappointment with Him. For the Christian, joy and peace come from reconciliation with God first and then with others. According to

Oswald Chambers, joy comes when we are fulfilling the purpose for which God created us, and doing so requires that we be reconciled to Christ in such a way that makes us:

> one in identity with the faith of Jesus, one in identity with the love of Jesus, one in identity with the Spirit of Jesus until we are so one in Him that the high-priestly prayer not only begins to be answered, but is clearly manifest in its answering—"that they may be one, even as We are."

Being one with Christ not only brings us into peace with God but gives us the actual peace of Christ. This peace is unshakeable. No trouble or conflict or crisis can take it from us. And that is pure joy.

Joy and peace throw their arms around us in celebration when we become one with Christ and then become reconciled to one another.

> *May the God of all peace grant us the joy of full participation in His plan of reconciling all things to Himself and restoring peace to planet earth.*

—Julie Ackerman Link

Joy

Strength *in the* LORD

The Benediction of Inspiration: We know that "the things which are not seen are eternal." Love, joy, peace are not seen, yet they are eternal, and God's nature is made up of these things.[PH]

Joy means the perfect fulfillment of that for which I was created and regenerated, not the successful doing of a thing. The joy our Lord had lay in doing what the Father sent him to do. We all have to find our niche in life and spiritually we find it when we receive our ministry from the Lord. In order to do this we must have companied with Jesus; we must know Him as more than a personal Savior. Have I received a ministry from the Lord? If so, I have to be loyal to it, to count my life precious only for the fulfilling of that ministry. COG

Reflection Questions

What is my spiritual niche? What am I doing that only I can do? What is my ministry from the Lord? Am I being loyal to it? In what way is my life precious to Jesus?

Lord, unto You do I come. Give me a gracious incoming of Your life till my reasoning, my imagination, and my speaking are all of You. How grandly You have renewed my spirit and restored to me the joy of Your salvation! KGD

There is no joy in a personality unless it can create. The joy of an artist is not in the fame which his pictures bring him, but that his work is the creation of his personality. The work of Jesus is the creation of saints. He can take the worst, the most misshapen material, and make a saint. The fullest meaning of sanctification is that Jesus Christ creates in us what He is Himself. The apostle Paul alludes to the joy of creating when he says, "For what is our hope, or joy, or crown of glorying? . . . For you are our glory and our joy."[BSG]

Reflection Questions

What has God called me to create? How does what I create reveal to others that God is creating in me the identity of Jesus?

The joy of Jesus was the absolute Self-surrender and Self-sacrifice of Himself to the will of His Father, the joy of doing exactly what the Father sent Him to do, and He prays that His disciples may have this same joy fulfilled in themselves.[BSG]

Have you ever been alone with Jesus? The disciples enjoyed the inestimable privilege not only of hearing the truth from Our Lord's own lips, but of questioning Him in secret about everything He said. The exposition the Holy Spirit will witness to is always so amazingly and profoundly simple that you feel, "Certainly that is God's truth." Whenever you are without that feeling about an interpretation, hesitate. Don't force your head to argue, but get alone with Jesus and ask Him. If He keeps you waiting, He knows why He does so. Discernment of God's truth and development in spiritual character go together.[AUG]

Reflection Questions

In what do I find more enjoyment: exploring theories about Jesus, examining interpretations of the Bible, or discerning God's truth by developing my spiritual character? What do I need to change?

When you have been "comforted by His rod and His staff," you count it all joy to go through this God-glorifying suffering.[CD]

In the natural world it is a real delight to be faced with risk and danger, and in the spiritual world God will plant us down among all kinds of people and give us the amazing joy of proving ourselves "a living sacrifice" in those circumstances. The Father's heart was thrilled with delight at the loyalty of His Son. Is Jesus Christ thrilled with delight at the way we are living a sacrificial life of holiness? The disciple has no program, only a distinguished passion of devotion to his Lord.[AUG]

Reflection Questions

What force propels me each day? On what is my life centered? Do I get more joy out of accomplishing a long list of tasks or from humbly acknowledging my limitations and allowing God to make my "to-do" list?

Self is not to be annihilated, but to be rightly centered in God. Self-realization has to be turned into Christ-realization. Our Lord taught that the principal purpose of our creation is "to glorify God and to enjoy Him forever"; that the sum total of my self is to be consciously centered in God.[BP]

What was the joy of the Lord Jesus Christ? His joy was in having completely finished the work His Father gave Him to do; and the same type of joy will be granted to every man and woman who is born of God and sanctified, when they fulfill the work God has given them to do. What is that work? To be a saint, a walking, talking, living, practical epistle of what God Almighty can do through the Atonement of the Lord Jesus Christ—one in identity with the faith of Jesus, one in identity with the love of Jesus, one in identity with the Spirit of Jesus until we are so one in Him that the high-priestly prayer not only begins to be answered, but is clearly manifest in its answering—"that they may be one, even as We are."[AUG]

Reflection Questions

In what ways do I try to find joy when I am not walking and talking like Jesus? What makes me think this is possible?

Job gives expression to a new conception of God; his hope is that an umpire will arise who will not only justify God, but also justify him. It was grief that brought Job to this place, and grief is the only thing that will; joy does not, neither does prosperity, but grief does.[BFB]

How anxious we are to serve God and our fellow men! Jesus our Lord says we must pay attention to the Source—believe in Him, and He will look after the outflow. He has promised that there shall be rivers of living water, but we must not look at the outflow, nor rejoice in successful service. "Rejoice not, that the spirits are subject unto you; but rather rejoice, because your names are written in heaven" (Luke 10:20 kjv). Belief in Jesus is the thing to heed; and through that commission, believers in Jesus are to make disciples.[AUG]

Reflection Questions

Do I know the authentic joy of having my name written in heaven? How often do I settle for the false joy of ecstasy or excitement? What keeps me from enjoying the wonderful condition of God's salvation?

When a man or woman realizes what God does work in them through Jesus Christ, they become almost lunatic with joy in the eyes of the world. It is this truth we are trying to state—the realization of the wonderful salvation of God.[ITWBP]

It is always easy to neglect a man or woman who deliberately accepts the aim of his life from the Lord Jesus. Many of us are imitators of other people; we do Christian work because someone has asked us to do it. We must receive our ministry, which is to testify the gospel of the grace of God, from Jesus Christ Himself, not from other Christians. Joy is the result of the perfect fulfillment of what a man is created for. It is continually necessary to revert to what the New Testament asks us to accept about ourselves. Our first accepted vocation is not to help men, but to obey God, and when we accept that vocation we enter into relationship with the despised and the neglected.[PR]

Reflection Questions

Do I imitate other people to avoid finding my own ministry? What testimony has God given to me and to no one else? What message of joy has God given me to proclaim?

God is so immediately near and so immensely strong that I get more and more joyous in my confidence in Him and less and less careful how I feel.[RTR]

The people who have plenty of time for you are those who have been through suffering, but now seem full of joy. If a man has not been through suffering he will snub you unless you share his interests, he is no more concerned about you than the desert sand; but those who have been through things are not now taken up with their own sorrows, they are being made broken bread and poured-out wine for others. You can always be sure of the man who has been through suffering, but never of the man who has not.[BFB]

Reflection Questions

Am I willing to forgo every other interest to identify myself with Jesus Christ's interests in other people? What sorrow have I experienced that has prepared me to spread the joyous news "that we may be perfect in Christ Jesus"?

The joy of God remained with Jesus, and He said, "I want My joy to be in you." The wonder of communion is that I know and believe that Jesus Christ has redeemed the world; my part is to get men to realize it and then devote themselves to Jesus.[HSGM]

People are tired of the preaching about a future heaven and they have gone to the other extreme and deal only with what is called the practical. Consequently they rob themselves of the unfathomable joy of knowing that everything God has said will come to pass. The Redemption covers more than men and women, it covers the whole earth. Everything that has been marred by sin and the devil has been completely redeemed by Jesus Christ. At present that is absolutely inconceivable to us. The world represents the societies of men on God's earth, and they do as they like; the earth remains God's. "Blessed are the meek: for they shall inherit the earth." The meek bide God's time.[BE]

Reflection Questions

Is my heart resting in the certainty that God is full of joy even though my experience is clouds and darkness? Is my confidence in Christ's final victory sufficient to sustain my joy while awaiting the fulfillment of His promise?

We go to God when we have no joy in ourselves and find that His joy is our strength.[THG]

Our Lord teaches that moral progress must start from a point of moral innocence, and is consequently only possible to a man when he has been born again. To become "as little children" means to receive a new heredity, a totally new nature, the essence of which is simplicity and confidence toward God. To develop the moral life, innocence must be transformed into virtue by a series of deliberate choices in which present pleasure is sacrificed for the ultimate joy of being good. The natural has to be transformed into the spiritual by willing obedience to the word and will of God.[BE]

Reflection Questions

What present pleasures do I need to sacrifice for the sake of ultimate joy? What deliberate choices do I need to make to transform my natural inclinations into spiritual innocence? What excesses do I use to cover up my lack of joy?

People noisy in words are not always turbulent in spirit; excessively quiet people who have nothing to express in shouting, may be joyous in heart.[IYSA]

Happiness is the portion of a child. Children ought to be thoughtless and happy, and woe to the people who upset their happiness. But if you take happiness as the end and aim for men and women you have to make its basis a determined ignorance of God. The seventy-third Psalm is the description of the man who has made happiness his aim. He is not in trouble as other men, neither is he plagued like other men; he has more than heart could wish. But once let his moral equilibrium be upset by conviction of sin and all his happiness is destroyed. The end and aim of human life is not happiness, but "to glorify God and enjoy Him forever." Holiness of character, chastity of life, living communion with God—that is the end of a man's life, whether he is happy or not. Happiness is no standard because happiness depends on being determinedly ignorant of God and His demands. Anything that relieves us from the individual responsibility of being personally related to God is corrupt.[BE]

Reflection Questions

How does my desire for happiness keep me ignorant of God? How is my pursuit of joy sabotaged by my desire for happiness?

God did not create Adam holy. He created him innocent, that is, without self-consciousness before God. Adam was conscious of himself only in relation to the Being whom he was to glorify and enjoy. Consciousness of self was an impossibility in the Garden until the introduction of sin. Sin kills the child in us and creates in us the bitter sinner. That is why our Lord says we have to become children all over again. In other words, God's right to me is killed by the incoming of my self-conscious right to myself. Sin is not a creation; it is a relationship set up between the devil (who is independent of God) and the being God made to have communion with Himself. Disobey God, separate yourself from Him, and you will be "as God, knowing good and evil" (Genesis 3:5 rv; see Genesis 3:22). The entrance of sin meant that the connection with God was gone and the disposition of self-realization had come in its place.ᴮᴱ

Reflection Questions

What "adult" attitudes do I need to sacrifice to regain childlikeness? Which parts of my "self" are keeping me from enjoying full communion with God?

The Psalmist states that wherever he may go in accordance with the indecipherable Providence of God, there the surprising presence of God will meet him. As soon as you begin to forecast and plan for yourself God will break up your program. He delights to do it, until we learn to live like children based on the knowledge that God is ruling and reigning and rejoicing, and His joy is our strength.[BE]

Reflection Questions

How does my need for a detailed plan for each day thwart God's desire to restore my childlike trust in His ability to rule and reign? What is God doing to awaken me from lethargy?

We rejoice in the presence of the Lord, we wait in hope for the revelation of the Lord Jesus Christ from heaven. The Holy Ghost is seeking to awaken men out of lethargy; He is pleading, yearning, blessing, pouring benedictions on men, convicting and drawing them nearer, for one purpose only, that they may receive Him so that He may make them holy men and women exhibiting the life of Jesus Christ.[BE]

I have no business to stir up the hatred of the world through a domineering religious opinion. That has nothing whatever to do with the spirit of Jesus. I am never told to rejoice when men separate me from their company on that account; but when in all modesty I am standing for the honor of Jesus Christ and a crisis arises when the Spirit of God requires that I declare my other-worldliness, then I learn what Jesus meant when He said, men will hate you.[BE]

Reflection Questions

Am I known for having strong opinions or strong faith? Do I put more energy into being right or being righteous? Would I rather stand up in support of a cause or for the honor of Jesus?

O God, increase my sense of You and my sensible understanding of Your Son, my Lord and Master. Grant that I may more and more realize Your dominance and rule, and more and more rejoice in simple joy in You.[KGD]

Some people take on the characteristic of always being merry and think they must always keep up that role. Others take on the role of being great sufferers, and never turn from it. Versatility is the power to turn from one thing to another. In the natural world it is called humor. Sin destroyed this power in the people of God. They forgot what God had done in the past; they had no power to turn from their present trying circumstances to the time when their circumstances were not trying. Consequently they sinned against God by unbelief. We have the power to turn from deep anguish to deep joy.[BP]

Reflection Questions

Does the expression on my face match the attitude of my heart? Am I more likely to hide the condition of my life from others than I am to hide myself in the life of Christ?

What a joyous life the life "hid with Christ in God" is! But, my God, I dare not for one moment think how far short of it I fall in spite of all Your grace and patience. But You are making me, and I thank You.[KGD]

If your circumstances are trying just now, remember the time when they were not trying, and you will be surprised at the self-righting power in the human heart to turn from one thing to another. How much misery a human heart can stand, and how much joy! If we lose the power of turning from one to the other, we upset the balance. God's Spirit restores and keeps the balance right.[BP]

Reflection Questions

Do I settle for cheerfulness instead of joy?
Is my confidence in God sufficient that I can
experience joy even during times of sorrow? Is
my experience of grace greater than my sin?

Preaching the gospel of "cheer up," when a person cannot cheer up. Telling him to look on the bright side of things when there is no bright side is as ridiculous as telling a jelly-fish to listen to one of Handel's Oratorios. It is just as futile to tell a man convicted of sin to cheer up. What he needs is the grace of God to alter him and put in him the well-spring of joy.[BP]

All degrees of joy reside in the heart. How can a Christian be full of happiness (if happiness depends on the things that happen) when he is in a world where the devil is doing his best to twist souls away from God, where people are tortured physically, where some are downtrodden and do not get a chance? It would be the outcome of the most miserable selfishness to be happy under such conditions. But a joyful heart is never an insult, and joy is never touched by external conditions.[BP]

Reflection Questions

What is the ratio of joy to happiness in my life? How often do I allow circumstances to determine my mood? How often am I joyful?

The Bible talks plentifully about joy, but it nowhere speaks about a "happy" Christian. Happiness depends on what happens; joy does not. Remember, Jesus Christ had joy, and He prays "that they might have My joy fulfilled in themselves."[BP]

Beware of preaching the gospel of temperament instead of the Gospel of God. Numbers of people today preach the gospel of temperament, the gospel of "cheer up." The word "blessed" is sometimes translated "happy," but it is a much deeper word; it includes all that we mean by joy in its full fruition. As men and women we should be facing the stern issues of life, knowing that the grace of God is sufficient for every problem the devil can present.[BP]

Reflection Questions

Do I crave cheerfulness or am I content with God's blessings? Am I trapped in an endless pursuit of happiness or liberated by the constant presence of joy and gladness?

Lord, today let Your praise abound, let joy and gladness resound everywhere. How I long for joy—great bounding liberating joy: joy in God, joy in the Holy Ghost, joy in life, and joy in love. Cause this to be a joyous house today, all day.[KGD]

When a man is happy, he cannot pull a long face. When he is happy inside he shows it on the outside. If you hear a Christian with a sad face saying, "Oh, I am so full of the joy of the Lord," well, you know it is not true. If I am full of the joy of the Lord, it will pour out of every cell of my body. The spirit of wrong shows itself in the flesh, and, thank God, the Spirit of God does the same.[BP]

Reflection Questions

Do I have an honest face? Not a face that causes people to trust me, but a face that allows people to see my true spiritual condition? Am I faking joy? What will it take to make it real?

If you become exhausted in doing work in the world, what have you to do? You have to take an iron tonic and have a holiday. But if you are exhausted in God's work, all the iron tonics in the world will never touch you. The only thing that will recuperate you is God Himself. Paul said he did not count his life dear unto himself so that he might finish his course with joy.[BP]

It was not reward our Lord looked forward to, but joy. "Reward" is our lame word for joy. When we want a child to do well, we do not say, "You will have joy"; we say, "You will have a reward, a prize." The way the joy of Jesus manifests itself is that there is no desire for praise. As Bergson has pointed out, we only want praise when we are not sure of having done well. When we are certain we have done well, we don't care whether or not folk praise us.[BSG]

Reflection Questions

What reward do I expect from others for fulfilling my role in God's plan? Am I disappointed when I receive no commendation? If I need the approval of other people how likely is it that I will ever experience true joy?

Lord, I praise You for the joy of my life here, for the favors of the Holy Spirit. What a wonder of joy and radiant blessing this place has been![KGD]

It is a wonderful thing to see a man or woman live in the light of something you cannot see. You can always tell when a person has an invisible standard; there is something that keeps them sweet when from every other consideration they ought to be sour. That is a mark of the Christian. He does not drift during times of peril. He has an anchor that holds within the veil. When we know that a time is coming when all things shall be explained fully, it keeps our spirit filled with uncrushable joy.[PH]

Reflection Questions

How does knowing the one who holds the future keep me from drifting into despair? What light do I need to focus on to stay on the journey of joy? Where do I need to place my anchor to keep from drifting off course?

O Lord God, what You are to me I dimly begin to discern—more than morning light, more than joy and health, more than all Your blessings. Dawn on me afresh this morning and make me light all through with Your light.[KGD]

From intellectual conviction and moral surrender to identification with the very life and joy of Jesus. A great thinker has said, "The seal and end of true conscious life is joy," not pleasure, nor happiness. Jesus said to His disciples, "These things have I spoken unto you, that My joy might remain in you, and that your joy might be full"— identity with Jesus Christ and with His joy.^AUG

Reflection Questions

How do I know if my joy is more than a state of mind? What does lack of joy tell me about my belief in God? What is the difference between having ideas about God and being identified with Jesus?

Many Christians get depressed over mean, despicable things they find in themselves. If we stake our all in Him, He will see us through as Savior or as Deliverer just where we need Him. It is a great thing to have a God big enough to believe in. The God revealed in Jesus Christ is grand enough for every problem of life. "I am the way, the truth, and the life." Let us carry away the Great Life of joy and simplicity.^AUG

What kind of Lord Jesus have we? Is He the all-powerful God in our present circumstances, in our providential setting? Is He the all-wise God of our thinking and our planning? Is He the ever-present God, closer than breathing, nearer than hands or feet? If He is, we know what it means to abide under the shadow of the Almighty. No one can tell us where the shadow of the Almighty is; we have to find it out for ourselves. When by obedience we have discovered the shadow of the Almighty we must abide there, for "there shall no evil befall thee, neither shall any plague come nigh thy dwelling." That is the life that is more than conqueror because the joy of the Lord has become its strength, and that soul is on the way to entering ultimately into the joy of the Lord.BSG

Reflection Questions

Have I found the safe place of the shaodow of the Almighty or am I hiding under something that keeps moving away from me?

An æsthete bases all his thinking on the principle that anything that produces joy is justifiable for him. Æstheticism may be all very well for the kingdom of heaven, but it is the doctrine of the devil himself for the kingdom of earth. If once you base your thinking on the principles of æstheticism, you can justify any kind of vile corruption. The test of every system of thinking is not how it works in the best case, but how it works in the worst case. If the test were the best cases, that is, if everyone were well brought up, if men and women had not a moral twist, then any of these philosophies would work out quite well. The miracle of the Redemption of Jesus Christ is that He can take the worst and the vilest of men and women and make saints out of them.[BSG]

Reflection Questions

What behaviors do I justify on the basis of how they make me feel? In what ways do I put my own feelings ahead of others? If I am primarily concerned about making myself feel good, how can I expect to experience true joy?

We take our salvation and our sanctification much too cheaply. We ought to rejoice when a man says he is saved, but remember what it cost God to make His grace a free gift. It cost agony we cannot begin to understand. The Christian faith means that the historic Cross of Christ is the pinhole in actual history through which we get a view of the purpose of God all through.[BSG]

Reflection Questions

How long has it been since the joy of being related to Jesus was the only joy I needed? How does being related to Christ change my view of the world?

Jerusalem stands in the life of our Lord as the place where He reached the climax of His Father's will. "I seek not My own will, but the will of the Father who has sent Me." That was the one dominating interest all through our Lord's life, and the things He met with on the way, joy or sorrow, success or failure, never deterred Him from His purpose. "He steadfastly set His face to go to Jerusalem."[COG]

When the disciples came back from their first mission, they were filled with joy because the devils were subject to them, and Jesus said—"Don't rejoice in successful service; the great secret of joy is that you are rightly related to Me." The great essential of the missionary is that he remains true to the call of God and realizes that his one purpose is to disciple men and women to Jesus.[COG]

Reflection Questions

Does my relationship with Jesus bring me joy? Why or why not? Am I bringing others into relationship with Jesus? What makes God joyful? How does His joy make me strong?

Am I certain that God is not miserable? Then His joy will be my strength. We are changed by looking to Jesus, not by introspection.[CD]

When we carry our religion as if it were a headache, there is neither joy nor power nor inspiration in it, none of the grandeur of the unsearchable riches of Christ about it, none of the passion of hilarious confidence in God. There is nothing in it of the robust strength of confidence in God which will go through anything, and stake its all on the honor of Jesus Christ. Christianity is the vital realization of the unsearchable riches of Christ.[PH]

Reflection Questions

Why do I become weary in well-doing? Why do I get headaches from serving the Lord? Am I so busy fighting human poverty that I am failing to explore the unsearchable riches of Christ?

Weariness sometimes comes in well-doing, when everything becomes listless. What is the cure? The cure is that of a right vision. Every man has the power to slay his own weariness, not by "bucking up" as you do physically, but by suddenly looking at things from a different standpoint. It is a tremendous thing to know that God reigns and rules and rejoices, and that His joy is our strength. The confidence of a Christian is that God never sulks.[PH]

Sin, suffering, and sanctification are not problems of the mind, but facts of life—mysteries that awaken all other mysteries until the heart rests in God. Oh, the unspeakable joy of knowing that God reigns, that He is our Father, and that the clouds are but "the dust of His feet"! Religious life is based and built up and matured on primal implicit trust, transfigured by Love; the explicit statement of that life can only be made by the spectator, never by the saint.[CD]

Reflection Questions

Do the difficulties, inequities, and mysteries of life cause me to give up in despair or convince me to trust the One who sends me out to proclaim the message that Love will conquer sin and suffering?

Lord, how little nourishment I have been giving to the indwelling Christ in me; O Lord, forgive me. Fill me with the ample sense of Your forgiveness that I may not only joy in Your salvation, but be filled with Your Spirit for the work here.[KGD]

If music turns the human heart into a vast capacity for something as yet undreamt of till all its being aches to the verge of infinity; if the minor reaches of our music have awakened harmonies in spheres we know not, till with dumb yearnings we turn our sightless orbs, "crying like children in the night, with no language but a cry"; if painters' pictures stop the ache which Nature started, and fill for one amazing moment the yearning abysses discovered by the more mysterious thing than joy in music's moments—it is but for a moment, and all seems but to have increased our capacity for a crueller sensitiveness, a more useless agony of suffering. But when God's servants guide us to His heart, then the first glorious outlines of the meaning of it all pass before us.[CD]

Reflection Questions

Do I rely on music to deliver joy to my soul from some external source, or do I use music to express the joy that's overflowing in my heart?

Too often we imagine that God lives in a place where He only repairs our broken treasures, but Jesus reveals that it is quite otherwise; He discerns all our difficulties and solves them before us. We are not beggars or spiritual customers; we are God's children, and we just stay before Him with our broken treasures or our pain and watch Him mend or heal in such a way that we understand Him better. The revelation here is of the free kingdom of love; there is no blind creaturely subjection to a Creator, but the free kingdom in which the one who prays is conscious of limit only through the moral nature of the Father's holiness. It is a revelation of pure joyousness in which the child of God pours into the Father's bosom the cares which give pain and anxiety so that He may solve them.[CD]

Reflection Questions

Have I learned the joy of expressing to God all my sorrow? Have I experienced the joy of seeing the Lord repair my broken treasures?

It is not our earnestness that brings us into touch with God, nor our devotedness, nor our times of prayer, but our Lord Jesus Christ's vitalizing death; and our times of prayer are evidences of reaction on the reality of Redemption, so we have confidence and boldness of access into the holiest. What an unspeakable joy it is to know that we each have the right of approach to God in confidence. What an awe and what a wonder of privilege, "to enter into the holiest," in the perfectness of the Atonement, "by the blood of Jesus."ᶜᴰ

Reflection Questions

How often do I rely on my own earnestness as a measure of my spirtual devotion? How often does joy come from God's ultimate triumph rather than my temporal success?

Look at such words as "power," "glory," "forever," "Amen." In them are sounds of transcendant triumphant truth that all is well, that God reigns and rules and rejoices, and His joy is our strength. What a rapturous grammar class our Lord Jesus conducts when we go to His school of prayer and learn of Him!ᶜᴰ

In all the temptations that contend in our hearts, and amid the things that meet us in the providence of God which seem to involve a contradiction of His Fatherhood, the secret place convinces us that He is our Father and that He is righteousness and love, and we remain not only unshaken but we receive our reward with an intimacy that is unspeakable and full of glory. Think of the unfathomable bliss of the revelation that we shall perceive our Father solving our problems, and shall understand Him; it is the reward of the joyous time of prayer.[CD]

Reflection Questions

Where is my secret place with God? What happens to my doubt and confusion when I don't go there? What happens to my joy when I do?

Lord, the hilarious simplicity of trust in You seems almost levity. Spread joy and gladness all around us this day.[KGD]

In the early days of spiritual experience we walk more by sight and feelings than by faith. The comforts, the delights, the joys of contact are so exquisite that the very flesh itself tingles with the leadings of the cloudy pillar by day and the fiery pillar by night. But there comes a day when all that ceases. Interior desolations serve a vital purpose in the soul of a Christian. It is expedient that the joys of contact be removed so that our idea of the Christian character may not be misplaced.[CD]

Reflection Questions

How far along am I in my spiritual journey? Am I still in the days of youthful exuberance or in the dark days of interior desolation? Will I stay on the journey of faith even when it leads me out of ecstasy? Do I worship God or my experience?

Whenever you make a transaction with God, it is real instantly and you have the witness; when there is no witness, no humility, no confidence or joy, it is because you have made a transaction with your religious self. That is self-idolatry; there is no trust in God in it.[NKW]

The real enjoyment of things seen and temporal is possible to the saint alone because he sees them in their true relationship to God. The sickening emptiness of the worldly minded who grasp the things seen and temporal as though they were eternal is unknown to him. The characteristic of the saint is not so much the renunciation of the things seen and temporal as the certainty that these things are but the shows of reality. The patience of hope does not turn men and women into monks and nuns; it gives them the right to use this world from another world's standpoint.[CD]

Reflection Questions

How does my attitude toward "things" affect my joy? How might I use things to bless others on God's behalf?

O Lord, this day keep us so well that we never need to think of ourselves at all, but joyously spend and be spent for You.[KGD]

The judgments of God leave scars, and the scars remain until I humbly and joyfully recognize that the judgments are deserved and that God is justified in them. The last delusion God delivers us from is the idea that we don't deserve what we get. Once we see ourselves under the canopy of God's overflowing mercy we are dissolved in wonder, love, and praise. That is the meaning of repentance, which is the greatest gift God ever gives a man.[CHI]

Reflection Questions

In what ways has repentance been a gift to me? From what have I turned away in pursuit of God and His holiness? What difference has it made?

The depth of possible sin is measured by the height of possible holiness. When men come under conviction of sin by the Holy Spirit their beauty is consumed. The misery which conviction brings enables a man to realize what God created him for: to glorify God and enjoy Him for ever.[CHI]

God expects His love to be manifested in our redeemed lives. We make the mistake of imagining that service for others springs from love of others; the fundamental fact is that love for our Lord alone gives us the motive and power to serve others. That means I have to identify myself with God's interests in other people, and God is interested in some extraordinary people. He is just as interested in the person you dislike as He is in you.[CHI]

Reflection Questions

How often is my service to others an expression of my love for God? How often is it an attempt to earn the love of God or to prove my love for God?

There is a distinction between the begging which knows no limit and the prayer which is conscious that there are limits set by the holy character of God. Repetition in intercessory importunity is not bargaining, but the joyous insistence of prayer.[NKW]

The fortune of misfortune! That is Paul's way of looking at his captivity. He does not want them to be depressed on his account, or to imagine that God's purpose has been hindered; he says it has not been hindered, but furthered. The very things that looked so disastrous have turned out to be the most opportune, so that on this account his heart bounds with joy, and the note of rejoicing comes out. CHI

Reflection Questions

What disasters have turned into opportunities?
What joy would I have missed if I had not walked with God through adversity?

The spirit of obedience gives more joy to God than anything else on earth. When the love of God is shed abroad in my heart (Romans 5:5), I am possessed by the nature of God, and I know by my obedience that I love Him. The best measure of a spiritual life is not its ecstasies, but its obedience.NKW

In talking to people you will be amazed to find that they much more readily listen if you talk about suffering the attacks of the devil; but get on the triumphant line of the apostle Paul, talk about the super-conquering life, about God making all His Divine grace to abound, and they lose interest, saying, "That is all in the clouds," a sheer indication that they have never begun to taste the unfathomable joy that is awaiting them if they will only take it. All the great prevailing grace of God is ours for the drawing on, and it scarcely needs any drawing on. Take out the "stopper" and it comes out in torrents; and yet we just manage to squeeze out enough grace for the day.[GW]

Reflection Questions

How much of my time do I spend talking about what's wrong with the world instead of what's great about God? Why is my experience of grace so meager?

A joyous, humble belief in your message will compel attention.[DI]

God's blessings fall, like His rain, on evil and good alike. The great blessings of health, genius, prosperity, all come from His overflowing grace, and not from the condition of the character of the recipients. For instance, if health were a sign that a man is right with God, we should lose all distinction as to what a good character is, for many bad men enjoy good health.[GW]

Reflection Questions

How does adversity affect my joy? Do I measure God's love by His blessings to me?

There is a difference between environment and circumstances. Every man has his own environment; it is that element in his circumstances which fits his disposition. We each make our own environment, our personality does it for us. Happiness means we select only those things out of our circumstances that will keep us happy. It is the great basis of false Christianity. The Bible nowhere speaks about a "happy" Christian; it talks plentifully of joy. Happiness depends on things that happen. Joyfulness is never touched by external conditions.[SA]

Solomon had everything a man could have in life, he had every means of satisfying himself; he tried the beastly line, the sublime line, the aesthetic line, the intellectual line but, he says, you cannot find your lasting joy in any of them. Joy is only to be found in your relationship to God while you live on this earth, the earth you came from and the earth you return to. Dust is the finest element in man, because in it the glory of God is to be manifested.SHH

Reflection Questions
What more do I think I need to attain joy?
What does it mean to delight in God's
creation? Why do I consider dust
a curse rather than a blessing?

What God created is a satisfaction to God, but until we come to know Him there is a great deal in His creation we shrug our shoulders over. Once we come to understand God we are as delighted with His creation as He is Himself. A child enjoys what God created, everything is wonderful to him.GW

At the outset of the Christian career the blessing of God is so sensible, so marked by feeling, that the Christian walks more by sight than by faith, God's caressings seem to be upon him. But there comes a time in the life of the disciple when God withdraws these comforts, when joy in God is not what it used to be, when His presence is not so sweet, and when a strange dull grey (if one might say so) seems to fall over the spiritual life. For a time the soul gets into deep darkness; then he begins to realize that God is but teaching him the difference between walking in the light of blessings and entering into the experience of the Divine beatitudes; or, to put it more simply, God is taking the soul out of the realm of religious feeling and emotion into the realm of faith.ᴳᵂ

Reflection Questions

In what ways is God teaching me to walk in the heavenly light of the Divine beatitudes rather than in the artificial light of earthly blessings?

I don't know what your natural heart was like before God saved you, but I know what mine was like. I was misunderstood and misrepresented; everybody else was wrong and I was right. Then when God came and gave me a spring-cleaning, dealt with my sin, and filled me with the Holy Spirit, I began to find an extraordinary alteration in myself. I still think the great marvel of the experience of salvation is not the alteration others see in you, but the alteration you find in yourself. When you come across certain people and things and remember what you used to be like in connection with them, and realize what you are now by the grace of God, you are filled with astonishment and joy; where there used to be a well of resentment and bitterness, there is now a well of sweetness. CHI

Reflection Questions

What change have I seen in myself since I started walking with God? What difference has God's grace made in my life?

One of the great marks that the blessings of God are being rightly used is that they lead us to repentance. How many of us have allowed the goodness of God to lead us to repentance? Or are we so enjoying the blessings of God, like the beasts of the field, taking them as our due and not seeing behind them the great loving hand of God, whose heart is overflowing in tremendous love?[GW]

Reflection Questions

When was the last time that an overwhelming sense of God's goodness called me to humble repentance? What might be the connection between that and my level of joy?

In every phase of human experience apart from Jesus, there is something that hinders our getting full joy. We may have the fulfillment of our ambitions, we may have love and money, yet there is the sense of something unfulfilled, something not finished, not right. A man is only joyful when he fulfills the design of God's creation of him, and that is a joy that can never be quenched.[HSGM]

Modern ethical teaching bases everything on the power of the will, but we need to recognize also the perils of the will. The man who has achieved a moral victory by the sheer force of his will is less likely to want to become a Christian than the man who has come to the moral frontier of his own need. When a man is stirred, either by joy or sorrow, he is apt to make vows which are beyond the possibility of human power to keep.^{GW}

Reflection Questions

If my goal is self-discipline and moral integrity what are my chances of attaining ultimate joy? Why? What vows have I made that require not just moral determination but supernatural intervention?

It takes a sharp discipline for many of us to learn that our goal is God Himself, not joy, nor peace, nor even blessing, but God Himself. Oh the joy of life with God and in God and for God!^{GW}

The first coming of Jesus into a life brings confusion, not peace (Matthew 10:34). When we receive the Holy Spirit the immediate manifestation is not peace and joy, but amazement, a sense of division instead of order, because we are being re-related to everything and seeing things differently. Before we received the Holy Spirit we used to have very clear and emphatic judgments. Now in certain matters we have not even ordinary common-sense judgment; we seem altogether impoverished. The way Jesus judges makes us know we are blind. We decide what is the most sensible common-sense thing to do, then Jesus comes instantly with His judgment and confuses everything, and in the end He brings out something that proves to be the perfect wisdom of God. The judgments of Jesus are always unexpected.HSGM

Reflection Questions

How has Jesus confused my common sense thinking? What judgments has He made that make no sense to me?

The realization that my strength is always a hindrance to God's supply of life is a great eye-opener. A man who has genius is apt to rely on his genius rather than on God. A man who has money is apt to rely on money instead of God. So many of us trust in what we have got in the way of possessions instead of entirely in God. All these sources of strength are sources of double weakness. But when we realize that our true life is "hid with Christ in God," that we are "complete in Him," in whom "dwells all the fulness of the Godhead bodily," then His strength is radiantly manifested in our mortal flesh. God grant that His Spirit may bring everyone of us to the place where the secret is learned and enjoyed that His strength is made perfect in our weakness.[GW]

Reflection Questions

How does my strength hinder God? How do my resources hinder God? What secret is being kept from me because I refuse to rely on God?

As in the natural world, so in the spiritual: knowledge is power. It is one thing to have participated in regeneration and sanctification and quite another thing to enjoy the knowledge that your body is "the temple of the Holy Ghost." That is not an experience, it is a revelation, and a revelation which takes some believing, and then some obeying. Let it dawn on your mind that your body is the temple of the Holy Ghost and instantly the impossible becomes possible.[HSGM]

Reflection Questions

What knowledge do I have that gives me power? What revelation have I received that makes the impossible possible? What chance does God have in my life?

Consciousness of sin is the exhaustion of sin, and is as big an alarm to the devil as it is a joy to the Holy Ghost. It is when we are not conscious of sin that condemnation is certain; when it spurts out in wrongs and immoralities, there is a chance for God.[NJ]

Joy is the great note all through the Bible. We have the notion of joy that arises from good spirits or good health, but the miracle of the joy of God has nothing to do with a man's life or his circumstances or the condition he is in. Jesus does not come to a man and say "Cheer up." He plants within a man the miracle of the joy of God's own nature.[HSGM]

Reflection Questions

What evidence do people see in my life that God has planted within me His joyous nature? Is my joy more often due to what God does for me or what God does within me?

The stronghold of the Christian faith is the joy of God not my joy in God. It is a great thing for a man to have faith in the joy of God, to know that nothing alters the fact of God's joy. God reigns and rules and rejoices, and His joy is our strength.[HSGM]

The miracle of the Christian life is that God can give a man joy in the midst of external misery, a joy which gives him power to work until the misery is removed. Joy is different from happiness, because happiness depends on what happens. There are elements in our circumstances we cannot help; joy is independent of them all.[HSGM]

Reflection Questions

Is my joy sufficient to survive times of misery?
In what ways is my joy superior to happiness?
When did I receive the nature of God and how is it being expressed in my life?

What was the joy of Jesus? That He did the will of His Father, and He wants that joy to be ours. Have I got the joy of Jesus, not a pumped-up ecstasy? The joy of Jesus is a miracle, it is not the outcome of my doing things or of my being good, but of my receiving the very nature of God.[HSGM]

What was the joy set before Jesus? The joy of bringing many sons to glory, not saved souls. It cost Jesus the Cross, but He despised the shame of it because of the joy that was set before Him. He had the task of taking the worst piece of broken earthenware and making him into a son of God. If Jesus cannot do that, then He has not succeeded in what He came to do. The badness does not hinder Him, and the goodness does not assist Him.[HSGM]

Reflection Questions

How often do I experience the joy of bringing souls to glory? What role does my joy play in repairing broken lives?

The Bible talks plentifully about joy, but it nowhere talks about a "happy Christian." Happiness depends on what happens; joy does not. Remember, Jesus Christ had joy, and He prays "that they might have My joy fulfilled in themselves."[RTR]

We can always know whether we are hearkening to God's voice by whether or not we have joy; if there is no joy, we are not hearkening. Hearkening to the voice of God will produce the joy that Jesus had. A life of intimacy with God is characterized by joy. You cannot counterfeit joy or peace. What is of value to God is what we are, not what we affect to be.[HSGM]

Reflection Questions

Is my joy real or pretend? Do I put it on like a forced smile or does it beat within me like my heart? Am I so devoted to my own ideas that I miss the joy of hearing God tell me His?

To be faithful in every circumstance means that we have only one loyalty, and that is to our Lord. Most of us are too devoted to our own ideas of what God wants even to hear His call when it comes. We may be loyal to what we like, but we may find we have been disloyal to God's calling of us by not recognizing Him in either the distress and humiliation or the joy and blessing.[HSGM]

It is a good thing to stoop as well as weep; there is more pride in human grief and misery than in joy and health; certain elements in human sorrow are as proud as the devil himself. There are people who indulge in the luxury of misery; they are always talking of the agonizing and distressing things. At the back of it is terrific pride, it is weeping that will not stoop.[HSGM]

Reflection Questions

What tempts me to indulge in the luxury of misery? What makes it so seductive? Why is misery an indication of pride? Why do tears not prove my humility?

The love of God is that He laid down His life for His enemies. Think of the worst man or woman you know; can you say to yourself, with any degree of joyful certainty, "That man, that woman—perfect in Christ Jesus"? You will soon see how much you believe in Christ Jesus and how much in common sense.[HSGM]

In certain stages of spiritual life we get the morbid conception that everything we have, we must give up. In the Bible the meaning of sacrifice is the deliberate giving of the best I have to God that He may make it His and mine for ever: if I cling to it I lose it, and so does God. God told Abraham to offer up Isaac for a burnt offering, and Abraham interpreted it to mean that he was to kill his son. But on Mount Moriah Abraham lost a wrong tradition about God and got a right insight as to what a burnt offering meant: a living sacrifice (Romans 12:1–2). It looks as if we had to give up everything, lose all we have, and instead of Christianity bringing joy and simplicity, it makes us miserable; until suddenly we realize what God's aim is that we have to take part in our own moral development, and we do this through the sacrifice of the natural to the spiritual by obedience, not denying the natural, but sacrificing it.HSGM

Reflection Questions

*What wrong concepts about God am I holding
on to that keep me from experiencing joy?*

Enchantment in the natural realm means to be taken out of your wits by song and rhythm; spiritual enchantment comes along the line of aggressive Christian work, meetings, and the contagion of other people's joy, and it is ensnaring. If we get taken up with salvation or with holiness or Divine healing instead of with Jesus Christ, we will be disillusioned. Many a man has found disillusionment when he is among men who do not care for his religion, and he finds there is not the thrill and the joy there used to be; he realizes he has been fostering a religious life which is not genuine, and spiritual cynicism may be the result. A cynic spiritually is one who cuts himself off from other people because the enchantment of service and association with others instead of producing reality has been engendering the attitude of a superior person.[HSGM]

Reflection Questions

Does my joy in Christ survive ridicule or disinterest from those who don't believe?

In a sermon on prayer, Scottish Old Testament scholar and ardent mountain climber Dr. George Adam Smith used an illustration from his own experience in Switzerland. As Smith neared the top of a certain mountain his guide stepped back to let him have the privilege of being first on the top. The exhilaration of the experience made him leap and jump for joy. Instantly the guide called out, "Down on your knees! It isn't safe standing up there."[HSGM]

Reflection Questions

Do I spend too much time in exuberant joy and shouting, forgetting that the only safe place is on my knees? In my eagerness to do God's will, do I neglect to ask Him what it is?

O Lord, how wholesome and grand a thing it is to be willing toward You. I am willing, eagerly willing for Your will to be done, and I feel all deeply joyful at the prospect for nothing can be so glorious as just Your will.[KGD]

Any soul who has no solitary place alone with God is in supreme peril spiritually. Have we allowed the solitary places to be broken down or built over with altars that look beautiful, and people passing by say, "How religious that person must be." Such an altar is an insult to the deep work of God in our souls. God grant we may learn more and more of the profound joy of getting alone with God in the dark of the night and toward the early dawn.[HSGM]

Reflection Questions

Where is my solitary place with God?
Do I enjoy being alone with God or am I eager to get to work? Do I begin every day by asking God what I should do and end it by asking how I did?

In the Book of Revelation, Jesus Christ refers to Himself as "the first and the last." It is in the middle that human choices are made; the beginning and the end remain with God. The decrees of God are birth and death, and in between those limits man makes his own distress or joy.[SHH]

Most of us are so shallow spiritually that when Our Lord in answer to some outrageous request we have made, asks us, "Are you able to drink the cup that I drink? or to be baptized with the baptism that I am baptized with?" We say, "We are able." Then He begins to show us what the cup and the baptism meant to Him, and there begins to dawn the great solemn day of martyrdom which closes for ever the day of exuberant undisciplined service, and opens the patient pilgrimage of pain and joy, with more of the first than the last.[HSGM]

Reflection Questions

Am I ready to receive from God the joy that comes not with happiness and ecstasy but with pain and weakness and humility?

O Lord, I beseech You for sustaining strength and simple joy. Keep me humble-minded in motive and design that nothing of the superior person may be mine.[KGD]

The first element in the life of faith is joy, which means the perfect fulfillment of that for which we were created. Joy is not happiness; there is no mention in the Bible of happiness for a Christian, but there is plenty said about joy. The next element is the realization that we have the delight of giving our lives as a love gift to Jesus Christ. Reward is the ultimate delight of knowing that God has fulfilled His purpose in my life; it is not a question of resting in satisfaction, but the delight of being in perfect conscious agreement with God.[HSGM]

Reflection Questions

Have I given my life as a love gift to God? Have I taken it back from Him when I didn't like how He was using it? Am I fulfilling God's purpose for my life or waiting for a second opinion?

Joy is not happiness, joy is the result of the perfect fulfillment of the purpose of the life. We never want praise if we have done perfectly what we ought to do; we only want praise if we are not sure whether we have done well. Jesus did not want praise; He did not need it.[SSIY]

Our Lord told His disciples to leap for joy "when men shall hate you, and when they shall separate you from their company, and shall reproach you and cast out your name as evil, for the Son of man's sake" (Luke 6:22–23). We are apt to look at this alternative as a supposition, but Jesus says it will happen and must be estimated. It is never wise to under-estimate an enemy. We look upon the enemy of our souls as a conquered foe, so he is, but only to God, not to us.THG

Reflection Questions

Am I more likely to feel joy when I am hated or loved? Have I ever been hated for my identification with Jesus? In what ways have I been deceived by the love of the world?

How my heart and my flesh cry out for the living God! Oh, the enervation of myself! and Oh, the refreshment and joy of the Lord!KGD

Ruskin says that early in life he could never see a hedgerow without emotion, then later on when problems of heart and life were busy with him he saw nothing in Nature; but as soon as the inner turmoil was settled, not only did he get the old joy back, but a redoubled joy. If we have no delight in God it is because we are too far away from the childlike relationship to Him. If there is an internal struggle on, get it put right and you will experience delight in Him.[THG]

Reflection Questions

Have I allowed earthly concerns to cloud my vision of God and make my soul numb to the joy and wonder of creation? What internal struggle is keeping me from experiencing delight in God's presence?

O Lord my God, my strength, my hope, and my joy, slowly but surely I seem to be emerging into a clearer discernment of You. Dawn through all earth-born clouds and mists today.[KGD]

Jesus Christ is not only Savior, He is King, and He has the right to exact anything and everything from us at His own discretion. We talk about the joys and comforts of salvation; Jesus Christ talks about taking up the cross and following Him. Very few of us know anything about loyalty to Jesus Christ. We look upon Jesus Christ as the best Example of the Christian life; we do not conceive of Him as Almighty God Incarnate, with all power in heaven and on earth. We make Him a comrade, One who in the battle of life has more breath than the rest of us and He turns round to lend a hand. We deal with Him as if He were one of ourselves; we do not take off the shoes from our feet when He speaks. Jesus Christ is Savior, and He saves us into His own absolute and holy lordship.[HSGM]

Reflection Questions

What joy have I found in sacrifice? Do I receive greater joy from having Jesus as a colleague than as King? Am I more joyful to think of ruling in God's kingdom or of suffering to further it?

The holiest person is not the one who is not conscious of sin, but the one who is most conscious of what sin is. The lower down we get into the experience of sin, the less conviction of sin we have. When we are regenerated and lifted into the light, we begin to know what sin means. The purer we are through God's sovereign grace, the more terribly poignant is our sense of sin. It is perilous to say, "I have nothing to do with sin now." Men living in sin don't know anything about it. Sin destroys the capacity of knowing what sin is. It is when we have been delivered from sin that we begin to realize by the pure light of the Holy Ghost what sin is. We shall find over and over again that God will send us shuddering to our knees every time we realize what sin is. When once the soul realizes what sanctification is, it is a joy unspeakable, but it is a joy in which there is the remembrance that the measure of your freedom from sin is the measure of your sense of what sin is.[THG]

Reflection Questions

What sin is so "normal" to me that I am unaware of it? What awareness of sin forgiven sends me to my knees in humble gratitude?

The great challenge in personal work is not simply that we realize the power of Jesus to save, but that we recognize the possibilities for evil in our own heart. It is impossible to discourage us because we start from a knowledge of Who Jesus Christ is in our own life. When we see evil and wrong exhibited in other lives, instead of awakening a sickening despair, it awakens a joyful confidence—I know a Savior who can save even that one.^{THG}

Reflection Questions

What awareness do I have of the potential for evil lurking in my life? What joy do I have in God's ability to forgive even the vilest offender? How does my own potential for wrong make me gracious to those still trapped in wrong-doing?

I would, O Lord, cleanse myself from all defilement of flesh and spirit, from every coarsening of the fiber of the spiritual life, so that I may dwell in the fulness of Your joy.^{KGD}

With regard to sin and misery. In the Bible you never find the note of the pessimist. In the midst of the most crushing conditions there is always an extraordinary hopefulness and profound joy, because God is at the heart. The effective working of Redemption in our experience makes us leap for joy in the midst of things in which other people see nothing but disastrous calamity.[THG]

Reflection Questions

Does my religious fanaticism woo people to Jesus with His joy and love or scare them away with my own judgmental attitudes?

The joy of the incoming grace of God always makes us fanatical. It is the potential position by grace, and God leaves us in that nursery of bliss just as long as He thinks fit, then He begins to take us on another step; we have to make that possible relationship actual. We have not only to be right with God inside, we have to be manifestly rightly related to God on the outside, and this brings us to the painful matter of discipline.[ITWBP]

The characteristic of many spiritual people today is intellectual intemperance, fanatical intoxication with the things of God, wild exuberance, an unlikeness to the sanity of Jesus in the very ways of God. There is a danger in the enjoyment of the delights and the power that come to us through Jesus Christ's salvation without lifting the life into keeping with His teaching, especially in spiritual people whose minds have never been disciplined.[ITWBP]

Reflection Questions

Is my joy founded on the truth of Jesus Christ and obedience to God's Word? Or is it an emotional response based on a misunderstanding of God's goodness? Does my praise give God reason to be joyful?

O Lord, I marvel at my slowness in praise; quicken me to praise You aright. Give me a due sense, a powerful realization of Your goodness, that I might be a joyous satisfaction to Your own heart.[KGD]

We receive our knowledge of the Holy Ghost not by experience first, but by the testimony of the Lord Jesus Christ. The testimony of Jesus Christ regarding the Holy Ghost is that He is here, and the real living experience the Holy Spirit works in us is that all His emphasis is laid on glorifying our Lord Jesus Christ. We know the Holy Spirit first by the testimony of Jesus, and then by the conscious enjoyment of His presence.[IYSA]

Reflection Questions

What have I learned about the Holy Spirit from the testimony of Jesus? How does His presence give me joy? What does it mean to me to know that God wants me to know Him?

God walked with man and talked with him, He told him His mind, and showed him the precise path in which he must walk in order to enjoy the happinesses He had ordained for him; He rejoiced in the fulness of His nature over man as His child, the offspring of His love. He left nothing unrevealed to man; He loved him. Oh, the joy and rapture of God the Father over man His son![LG]

God is love. In the future, when trial and difficulties await you, do not be fearful, whatever and whoever you may lose faith in, let not this faith slip from you—God is Love; whisper it not only to your heart in its hour of darkness, but here in your corner of God's earth and man's great city, live in the belief of it; preach it by your sweetened, chastened, happy life; sing it in consecrated moments of peaceful joy. The world does not bid you sing, but God does. Song is the sign of an unburdened heart; then sing your songs of love unbidden, ever rising higher and higher into a fuller conception of the greatest, grandest fact on the stage of Time.[LG]

Reflection Questions

What song does God bid me sing? What do my songs say about the burdens I carry and the love I have? How is my joy expressed in song?

O Lord, my Lord and Master, may I be so consciously Yours today that I am at home with You, and joyous in my childlike delight in Your possession of me.[KGD]

The strength of life is not in the certainty that we can do the thing, but in the perfect certainty that God will. We are certain only of the One Whom we are trusting. The strength of our life lies in knowing that our strength is in God. When we know the love of Christ, which passes knowledge, we are free from anxiety, free from carefulness, so that during the twenty-four hours of the day we do what we ought to do all the time, with the strength of life bubbling up with real spontaneous joy.[LG]

Reflection Questions

How does the love of Jesus relieve my anxiety? How am I strengthened by joy? Why is knowing that I can't achieve godliness through self-discipline a reason for joy?

Whenever we think we can get the life of God by obedience or prayer or some kind of discipline, we are wrong. This is not a sad statement, but a joyful one. We can only enter into the Kingdom of God if God will stoop down and lift us up. That is exactly what Jesus Christ promises to do.[LG]

The joy of Jesus lay in knowing that every power of His nature was in such harmony with His Father that He did His Father's will with delight. Some of us are slow to do God's will; we do it as if our shoes were iron and lead; we do it with a great sigh and with the corners of our mouths down, as if His will were the most arduous thing on earth. But when our wills are rectified and brought into harmony with God, it is a delight, a superabounding joy, to do God's will.[MFL]

Reflection Questions

Why am I slow to do God's will? What false belief makes me think that God doesn't want me happy? When have I experienced the delight of doing God's will?

Talk to saints about suffering and they look at you in amazement. "Suffering? What suffering?" Suffering is a matter of interpretation. For the saint it is an overwhelming delight in God; not delight in suffering, but if God's will should lead through suffering, there is delight in His will.[MFL]

Whenever the angels come to this earth they come bursting with a joy which instantly has to be stayed (cf. Luke 2:13). This earth is like a sick chamber, and when God sends His angels here He has to say— "Now be quiet; they are so sick with sin that they cannot understand your hilarity." Whenever the veil is lifted there is laughter and joy. These are the characteristics that belong to God and God's order of things; sombreness and oppression and depression are the characteristics of all that does not belong to God.[NKW]

Reflection Questions

What veil of false teaching keeps me from experiencing the joy of the Lord? When was the last time I was bursting with joy? How are creativity and joy related?

Every time we have transacted business with God on His covenant and have let go entirely on God, there is no sense of merit in it, no human ingredient at all, but such a complete overwhelming sense of being a creation of God's that we are transfigured by peace and joy.[NKW]

Measure your ultimate delight in God's truth and joy in God by the little bit that is clear to you. There are whole tracts of God's character unrevealed to us as yet, and we have to bow in patience until God is able to reveal the things which look so dark. The danger is lest we make the little bit of truth we do know a pinnacle on which we set ourselves to judge everyone else. It is perilously easy to make our conception of God like molten lead and pour it into our specially designed mould and then when it is cold and hard, fling it at the heads of the religious people who don't agree with us.[NI]

Reflection Questions

What is clear to me about God? Is it enough to make me joyful without making me judgmental? If all I know about God is all there is to know about God, what reason would I have for joy?

The realization of the election of grace by regeneration, and of being thereby perfectly fitted for glorifying God, is the most joyful realization.[NE]

When we trust God we suffer with joy because we know that every bit of God's truth is going to be as gladsome a delight to us as the little bit of truth we already know. All the terrors of God's processes in history do not alarm us, because the one bit we do know personally about God is so ineffably full of light and joy; therefore we can wait in patience.[NJ]

Reflection Questions

When I examine God's work in the past, what joy does it give me for the future? Do I spend more time examining myself than I do others? When I examine myself, do I find light or darkness? Why do I feel pleasure when I feel superior to someone else?

Self-examination is the only exercise for a soul who would remain true to the light of God. The hardest thing in a saint's life is to maintain a simple belief in Jesus until he realizes the one relationship is—my Lord and I; then His joy will be fulfilled in us.[NJ]

Doing God's will is never hard. The only thing that is hard is not doing His will. All the forces of nature and of grace are at the back of the man who does God's will. We ought to be super-abounding with joy and delight because God is working in us to will and to do of His good pleasure. God's will is hard only when it comes up against our stubbornness. When once God has His way, we are emancipated into the very life of God.ᴼᴮᴴ

Reflection Questions

Do I delight in doing God's will or do I consider it difficult? What makes me think that God would ask me to do anything that He won't equip and enable me to do?

Before a man is rightly related to God, his conscience may be a source of torture and distress to him, but when he is born again it becomes a source of joy and delight because he realizes that not only are his will and his conscience in agreement with God, but that God's will is his will, and the life is as natural as breathing.ᴼᴮᴴ

When men depart from the Bible, God is simply the name given to the general tendencies which further men's interests—that God and Jesus Christ and the Holy Ghost are simply meant to bless us, to further our interests. When we come to the New Testament we find exactly the opposite idea, that by regeneration we are brought into such harmony and union with God that we realize with great joy that we are meant to serve His interests.[PS]

Reflection Questions

Do I use God to further my own interests or do I serve God to further His? Do I use the Bible to prove that I am right or to find out where I am wrong? Am I joyful to find out where I am wrong so I can be made right?

If we keep in the light with God, our life is that of a child, simple and joyful all through. It is sufficient for a child to know that his father wishes him to do certain things and he learns to draw on a strength greater than his own.[PS]

When we see the awfulness of evil in this world we imagine there is no room for anything but the devil and wrong; but this is not so. God restrains the powers of evil. How does He do it? Through the lives of the saints who are pushing the battle everywhere their feet are placed. The devil tackles on the right hand and on the left but they are more than conquerors, they not only go through the tribulation, but are exceeding joyful in it.^{SHL}

Reflection Questions

How is God using me to restrain evil in the world? Am I joyfully cooperating or grumbling that I have go against popular opinion? Am I standing up for the truth of the gospel or falling for Satan's lies?

When we know the love of Christ, we are free from anxiety, free from carefulness, so that we do what we ought to do all the time, with the strength of life bubbling up with real spontaneous joy.^{RTR}

Speak about the peace of heaven and the joy of the Lord, and men will listen to you. But tell them that the Holy Spirit has to come in and turn out their claim to their right to themselves, and instantly there is resentment. The majority of people are not blackguards and criminals; they are clean-living and respectable. And it is to such that the scourge of God is the most terrible thing because it reveals that the natural virtues may be in idolatrous opposition to God.[SHL]

Reflection Questions

Am I willing to speak of things that upset people's sense of personal well being? Am I willing to confess when God reveals that my own peace and joy is based on feelings of self-righteousness?

You carry a wonderful kingdom within, a kingdom full of light and peace and joy no matter how destitute and alone you may be on the outside. That is the wonderful work of the Lord in a man's soul.[SHL]

There is no man without some spot in his life where there is something dear, something that is a truth to him, a real wonderful possession full of light and liberty and joy, the finest spot in his experience. Jesus Christ says that ultimately through patience and by deliberately going on with God, everything that is now obscure will be as clear as that one spot. If we "hang in" with patience, we shall see everything rehabilitated, and God will be justified in everything He has allowed.ᴿᴴᴴ

Reflection Questions

What truth do I know as certainly as I know my own name? What mystery am I waiting to be solved? Am I grumbling because I don't have all the answers or joyfully awaiting the great revelation?

Unless a man relates his disposition to God in between birth and death, he will reap a heritage of distress for himself and for those who come after him. The man who is banked on a real relationship to a personal God will reap not the distress that works death, but the joy of life.ˢᴴᴴ

There is such a thing as an obsession of solitariness. Hermits, ascetics, and celibates cut themselves off in revolt because they cannot find peace or joy or happiness in the tyranny of civilized life or in commerce. They cannot be idle tramps, so they become solitary and live sequestered lives. Solomon points out what history has proved: This experiment ends disastrously because a man cannot shut out what is inside by cutting himself off from the outside.[SHH]

Reflection Questions

Am I obsessed with solitariness? Do I believe that I can escape the influence of evil by avoiding contact with the world? Am I looking for joy in a place rather than a Person?

If only I could get away and be quiet; if only I could live in a sunrise or a sunset. We desire to be solitary, but we have to find our true life in things as they are—with that on the inside which keeps us right. The true energy of life lies in being rightly related to God, and only there is true joy found.[SHH]

Whether you are wise or foolish, upright or not, a king or tyrannized by a king, successful or a failure, in society or solitary, stubborn or sagacious, all alike ends the same way. All is passing, says Solomon, and we cannot find lasting joy in any element we like to touch. It is disastrous for a man to try and find his true joy in any phase of truth, or in the fulfillment of ambition, or in physical or intellectual solitariness, or in society; he will find his joy only in a personal relationship to God. Jesus Christ is God manifested in human flesh, and we have to ignore to the point of hatred anything that competes with our relationship to Him.[SHH]

Reflection Questions

In what places or positions have I tried to find joy? In what ambition, belief, or conviction have I expected to discover joy? In what human relationships have I looked for joy?

The true joy of a man's life is in his relationship to God, and the great point of the Hebrew confidence in God is that it does not unfit a man for his actual life. That is always the test of a false religion.[SHH]

You cannot find lasting joy in things, let them come and go, remain true to your relationship to God and don't put your trust in possessions. Live your life as a labouring man, a man rightly related to mother earth, and to the providential order of tyranny; trust in God whatever happens, and the result will be that in your heart will be the joy that every man is seeking.

Reflection Questions

How much joy have I lost in trying to follow rules imposed by other people? How much joy have I stolen from others by imposing my rules on them? What gift has God given to me that I have refused to enjoy?

The test that a man is right with God is in eating and drinking. Solomon says, "It is good and comely for men to eat and drink." Paul says, Beware of those who teach abstinence from meats. Remain true to God in your actual life. The right thing to do with riches is to enjoy your portion, and remember that what you lay by is a danger and a snare.SHH

You have to live this life with confidence based on God, and see that you keep your day full of the joy and light of life; enjoy things as they come. When we have a particularly good time, we are apt to say, "Oh well, it can't last long." We expect the worst. When we have one trouble, we expect more. The Bible counsels us to rejoice, yet remember the days of darkness.[SHH]

Reflection Questions

How often do I rob myself of joy with my anxiety about the future? What keeps me from seeing God's goodness even on the worst day? What keeps me from rejoicing in God's character even when circumstances

are uncertain?

Solomon prospected to find out where the true essential enjoyment of life lay. Was it in being an animal, an intellectualist, an aesthete, a governor, in being educated or uneducated? And he came to the conclusion that a man cannot find the true essential joy of his life anywhere but in his relationship to God.[SHH]

All through the books of Hebrew Wisdom there is this certainty that the basis of actual life is tragedy. Human nature is a ruin of what it once was, and a man is a fool to ignore that. If you want to know the basis of life, it is better to go to the house of mourning than to the house of pleasure. Remember, there is death, and there is worse than death—sin and tragedy and the possibility of terrible evil. Solomon is not implying that it is better to grouse around in the luxury of misery than to feast; he is dealing with finding true essential joy, and he says if ever we are going to have a true estimate of life we shall have to face it at its worst.[SHH]

Reflection Questions

Do I believe the best about God when I am witnessing the worst of life? In what situations has God showed me the joy of the Lord in the midst of misery?

Lord, I feel myself craving the external sense of Your presence, the hundredfold more of Your joyous benediction. Lord, I leave this desire with You. Grant it as You see best.[KGD]

There is nothing more irritating than the counsel, "keep smiling"; that is a counterfeit, a radiance that soon fizzles out. The one thing that Jesus Christ does for a man is to make him radiant, not artificially radiant. The joy that Jesus gives is the result of our disposition being at one with His own disposition. The Spirit of God will fill us to overflowing if we will be careful to keep in the light. We have no business to be weak in God's strength.[PH]

Reflection Questions

Is my smile forced or natural? Is my joy a hopeful pretense or inner radiance? Do I trust that God can give me joy through circumstances that I do not choose?

We have no business to tell God we cannot stand any more; God ought to be at liberty to do with us what He chooses, as He did with His own Son. Then whatever happens our life will be full of joy.[PH]

Glorying is the experience of joy on the inside, associated with the fame of God on the outside. Paul says his glorying is in the Cross of Christ. Joy is neither happiness nor brightness. Joy is the nature of God in my blood, no matter what happens. The joy that Jesus exhibited in His life was in knowing that every power of His nature was in harmony with His Father's nature. Therefore He did with delight what God designed Him for as Son of Man. Anything that exactly fulfills the purpose of its creation experiences joy, and Paul states that our joy is that we fulfill the purpose of God in our lives by being saints.[PR]

Reflection Questions

Is my nature in harmony with Jesus? Do I agree with God about what is good? Am I delighted when God's name is exalted? Is my desire aligned with God?

The agony of Jesus is the basis of the simplicity of our salvation. His suffering is the basis of all our light and liberty and joy. His Cross makes it simple enough for any one to get into the presence of God.[PR]

Joy & Peace: A Holy Condition

The Scriptures are full of admonitions to rejoice, to praise God, to sing aloud for joy; but only when one has a cause to rejoice, to praise, and to sing aloud can these things truly be done from the heart. In the physical realm the average sick man does not take a very bright view of life, and with the sick in soul true brightness and cheer are an impossibility. Until the soul is cured there is always an underlying dread and fear which steals away the gladness and unspeakable joy which God desires for all His children.^{WG}

Reflection Questions

What is my reason for rejoicing? From what sickness—physical or spiritual—have I been cured? From what discouragement have I been delivered? From what fear have I been freed?

Only when God takes a life in hand can there come deliverance from discouragement. Living in the peace and joy of God's forgiveness and favor is the only thing that will bring cheerfulness.^{WG}

The joy of the Lord Jesus Christ lay in doing exactly what He came to do. He did not come to save men first of all, He came to do His Father's will. The saving of men was the natural outcome of this, but Our Lord's one great obedience was not to the needs of men but to the will of His Father. We are never told to consecrate our gifts to God, but we are told to dedicate ourselves.[LG]

Reflection Questions

Am I more concerned about getting results or being obedient? Am I more likely to dedicate my gifts or myself? Do I allow affliction to destroy joy or do I see affliction as a means to joy?

If you are right with God, the very thing which is an affliction to you is working out an eternal weight of glory. The afflictions may come from good people or from bad people, but behind the whole thing is God. Whenever Paul tries to state the unfathomable joy and glory which he has in the heavenlies in Christ Jesus, it is as if he cannot find words to express his meaning.[LG]

Suppose Our Lord had measured His life by whether or not He was a blessing to others. Why, He was a "stone of stumbling" to thousands, actually to His own neighbors, to His own nation, because through Him they blasphemed the Holy Ghost, and in His own country "He did not many mighty works there because of their unbelief" (Matthew 13:58). If Our Lord had measured His life by its actual results, He would have been full of misery. We are not here to win souls, to do good to others; that is the natural outcome, but it is not our aim, and this is where so many of us cease to be followers. We will follow God as long as He makes us a blessing to others, but when He does not we will not follow. The joy of anything, from a blade of grass upward, is to fulfill its created purpose—that we should be to the praise of His glory."[LG]

Reflection Questions

How do I measure my life? Do I use God's measurements of faithfulness and godliness or the worldly values of popularity, productivity, and efficiency?

We get switched off when instead of following God we follow Christian work and workers. We are much more concerned over the passion for souls than the passion for Christ. The passion for Christ is the counterpart of His passion for God. The life of God is manifested in Our Lord Jesus Christ—He came to do His Father's will. The passion for souls is not a New Testament idea at all, but religious commercialism. When we are taken up with this passion the joy of the Lord is never ours, but only an excitable joy which always leaves behind a snare. When we are following Him, it will be a matter of indifference whether God puts us in the forefront or in the back seat. When we realize this, the joy of the Lord is ours because we are fulfilling our purpose.[LG]

Reflection Questions

Who do I follow? Is my faith more like religious commercialism than loving devotion? Does my joy come from being visible or invisible?

The strain on a violin string when stretched to the uttermost gives it its strength; and the stronger the strain, the finer is the sound of our life for God, and He never strains more than we are able to bear. We say, "sorrow, disaster, calamity." God says, "chastening," and it sounds sweet to Him though it is a discord to us. Patience has the meaning of testing—a thing drawn out and tested, drawn out to the last strand in a strain without breaking, and ending in sheer joy. Don't faint when you are rebuked, and don't despise the chastenings of the Lord. If God has given you a time of rest, then lie curled up in His leaves of healing.[LG]

Reflection Questions

Is the tension I feel due to God's patient work of getting me in tune with the other instruments in His orchestra? Am I willing to endure for the joy of making beautiful music?

God showed to man that compliance with His dictates would mean eternal bliss and joy unspeakable and life and knowledge for evermore. Ceasing to comply would mean loss of life with God and eternal death.[LG]

We have dragged down the idea of surrender and of sacrifice. We have taken the life out of the words and made them mean something sad and weary and despicable. In the Bible they mean the very opposite. Sacrifice in the Bible means that we give to God the best we have; it is the finest form of worship. Sacrifice is not giving up things, but giving to God with joy the best we have.[LG]

Reflection Questions

Am I willing to act on what I know so that the will of God may be performed in me? Am I willing to give to God the best I have so that I can receive from Him the best He has?

When the intention of an honest soul is grasped by the Spirit of God he will know whether the teaching Jesus gives is of God or not. To know that the teaching of Jesus is of God means that it must be obeyed. It may be difficult to begin with, but the difficulty will become a joy.[MFL]

We cannot calculate God, and that is the immense joy of Christian life. To be certain of God means that we are delightfully uncertain in all our ways, we do not know what a day may bring forth. That is generally said with a sigh of sadness, but it should be rather an expression of breathless unexpectedness. It is exactly the state of mind we should be in spiritually, a state of expectant wonder, like a child. When we are certain of God we always live in this delightful uncertainty; whereas if we are certain of our beliefs we become even-tenored people who never expect to see God anywhere.[LG]

Reflection Questions

Does the idea of an unpredictable God comfort me or trouble me? Why? What joy would be missing if all mystery were removed? Why is gradual realization more rewarding than complete revelation?

Undertake with Your easy power and might; graciously dawn on us physically and mentally and spiritually. Grant us light and sweetness and joy all day.[KGD]

The Bible nowhere teaches us to be uncompromising in our opinions. Jesus did not say, "Leap for joy when men separate you from their company for the sake of your convictions." He said, "Leap for joy when men cast out your name as evil, for the Son of Man's sake." I may be such a pig-headed cross-patch, and have such determined notions of my own, that no one can live with me. That is not suffering for the Son of Man's sake; it is suffering for my own sake. Never compromise with anything that would detract from the honor of the Lord. Remember that the honor of Jesus is at stake in your bodily life. Rouse yourself up to act accordingly.[MFL]

Reflection Questions

Do I take joy in forming strong convictions or in confessing my misguided notions? Am I willing to be labeled "evil" for the sake of identifying with Jesus?

In all matters, O Lord, I would acknowledge You. Keep us in tune with You that others may catch the joyousness and gladness of God.[KGD]

Step by step God teaches us what is His will; then comes a great burst of joy, "I delight to do Your will! There is nothing on earth I delight in more than in Your will." When we become rightly related to God we are the will of God in disposition, and we have to work out God's will; it is the freest, most natural life imaginable. There is no such thing as freedom in the world, and the higher we go in the social life the more bondage there is. Worldly people imagine that the saints must find it difficult to live with so many restrictions, but the bondage is with the world, not with the saints. MFL

Reflection Questions

Have I reached the place where I can say, "I delight to do Your will"? Have I discovered the freedom of doing only what God designed me to do? Have I experienced the relief of knowing God is all I need?

O Lord, with what abundant relief I turn to You, I need You in unfathomable ways, and with what amazed relief and joy I find all I need is You. KGD

Whenever there is the experience of weariness or degradation, you may be certain you have done one of two things—either you have disregarded a law of nature, or you have deliberately got out of touch with God. There is no such thing as weariness in God's work. If you are in tune with the joy of God, the more you spend out in God's service, the more the recuperation goes on, and when once the warning note of weariness is given, it is a sign that something has gone wrong. If only we would heed the warning, we would find it is God's wonderfully gentle way of saying, "Not that way; that must be left alone; this must be given up."[NKW]

Reflection Questions

What warning is my weariness sending me? Have I neglected God or disregarded His design and purpose for me? What is God telling me to give up? Where is He telling me not to go?

Lord, lift me up to You so that the bloom, the radiant joy of Your salvation, visits me and shines forth for Your glory. Keep me in flowing intercession with You.[KGD]

After an experience of sanctification, many try and serve two masters. They go into the joy of successful service, and slowly the eye becomes fixed on the sanctified "show business" instead of on Jesus Himself. The only illustrations our Lord used of service were those of the vine (John 15:1–6), and the rivers of living water (John 7:37–39). It is inconceivable to think of the vine delighting in its own grapes. Are we bringing forth fruit? We certainly are if we are identified with the Lord, luscious bunches of grapes. Pay attention to the Source, believe in Jesus, and God will look after the increase. MFL

Reflection Questions

What does success look like to me? Does it involve lights and cameras or streams and vines? Do I have the mind of Christ or the mind of my friends and colleagues?

God, grant that we may let the Holy Ghost work out His passion for souls through us. May we not try to imitate Jesus but to let the Holy Ghost so identify us with Jesus that His mind is expressed through us as He expressed the mind of God. MFL

Sanctification is Christ formed in us; not the Christ-life, but Christ Himself. In Jesus Christ is the perfection of everything, and the mystery of sanctification is that we may have in Jesus Christ, not the start of holiness, but the holiness of Jesus Christ. All the perfections of Jesus Christ are at our disposal if we have been initiated into the mystery of sanctification. No wonder men cannot explain this mystery for the joy and the rapture and the marvel of it all, and no wonder men see it when it is there, for it works out everywhere.OBH

Reflection Questions

Have I been initiated into the mystery of sanctification? How do I express my gratitude to God for showing me the way of life? What joy do I find in standing for what is right?

The people who influence us are those who have stood unconsciously for the right thing. They are like the stars and the lilies, and the joy of God flows through them all the time.HSGM

The first thing that happens after we have realized our election to God in Christ Jesus is the destruction of our prejudices and our parochial notions and our patriotisms; we are turned into servants of God's own purpose. Sin has not altered God's purpose in the tiniest degree; and when we are born again we are brought into the realization of God's great purpose for the human race. I am created for God. He made me. This realization of the election of God is the most joyful realization on earth, and we have to learn to rely on the tremendous creative purpose of God.cog

Reflection Questions

What prejudices and patriotisms did I give up when I realized my election by God for His purpose? Do I put more energy into promoting and sustaining an earthly kingdom or a spiritual kingdom?

We cannot do anything without our ruling disposition instantly being marked in it. We gain our point of distress or of joy by the way we use or misuse our twenty-four hours.shh

All that lies dark and obscure just now is one day going to be as clear, as radiantly and joyously clear, as the bit we have seen. No wonder God counsels us to be patient. Little by little everything will be brought into the light until we understand as Jesus Christ understood. The whole of Eternity will be taken up with understanding and knowing God, and, thank God, we may begin to know Him down here. The sanctified life means that we begin to understand God and to manifest the life of the Son of God in our mortal flesh.[OBH]

Reflection Questions

Do I enjoy God's slow-paced revelation or do I become impatient with His lack of urgency? If God is in no hurry, why am I? How can I enjoy knowledge if I don't enjoy discovery?

Every bit of knowledge that we have of God fills us with ineffable joy. If we understand God on any one point we will know something of the joy that Jesus had. It is a wonderful possession, it is the very characteristic of Jesus.[OBH]

The first moment of realizing God's truth is usually a moment of ecstasy. Life is brimming over with joy and happiness and brightness. There is no pain, nothing but unspeakable, unfathomable joy. Then the verb "to go" begins to be conjugated, and we experience the "growing pains" of salvation, and Satan comes as an angel of light and says, "Don't go on, stand still." We do not consider enough the necessity of learning how to walk spiritually. If a man has used his arm only for writing, and then becomes a blacksmith, he will groan for days until by practice the muscle has become rightly adjusted to its new work. The same thing happens spiritually, God begins to teach us how to walk and over and over again we begin to howl and complain. May God save us from the continual whine of spiritual babes. Thank God there is a pain attached to being saved, the pain of growing until we come to maturity where we can do the work of a son or daughter of God.[ps]

Reflection Questions

Have I reached the point of being able to find joy in the pain associated with gaining spiritual strength?

The nature of spiritual life is that we are certain in our uncertainty, consequently we do not make our "nests" anywhere spiritually. Immediately we make a "nest" out of an organization or a creed or a belief, we come across the biggest of all calamities, the fact that all certainty brings death. G. K. Chesterton, that insurgent writer, pronounces all certainties "dead certainties." Whenever I become certain of my creeds, I kill the life of God in my soul, because I cease to believe in God and believe in my belief instead. All through the Bible the realm of the uncertain is the realm of joy and delight; the certainty of belief brings distress. Certainty of God means uncertainty in life; while certainty in belief makes us uncertain of God.[LG]

Reflection Questions

What "certainties" do I need to put to death? What uncertainty should I welcome into my life? What joy do I lose when I cling to creeds instead of Christ?

Persecution is the thing that tests our Christianity, and it always comes in our own setting; the crowd outside never bothers us. To have brickbats and rotten eggs flung at you is not persecution, it simply makes you feel good and does you no harm at all. But when your own crowd cut you dead and systematically vex you, then says Jesus, "count it all joy." Leap for joy "when men shall hate you, and when they shall separate you from their company, and reproach you, and cast out your name as evil for the Son of man's sake" — not for the sake of some crotchety notion of our own.SHL

Reflection Questions

How have I experienced persecution from those related to me by family or faith? What did I do to make them turn against me? Did I feel joy while waiting for vindication?

O Lord, restore the unique joy of Your presence to me and make me Yours. I seem unsuited for anything but just waiting on You. Show me a token for good, O Lord. KGD

The only way we can enjoy our "tree of life" is by fulfilling the purpose of our creation. Jesus Christ prayed "that they may have My joy fulfilled in themselves." The thing that kept Jesus joyful was not that He held aloof from actual things, but that He had a kingdom within. Our Lord's whole life was rooted and grounded in God, consequently He was never wearied or cynical.SHH

Reflection Questions

What people cause me to be cynical? Why do I allow their values and choices to diminish my joy? When I allow cynicism, what does it tell me about my own values? What choices can I make to replace cynicism with joy?

Within the limits of birth and death I can do as I like; but I cannot make myself un-born, neither can I escape death, those two limits are there. I have nothing to do with placing the limits, but within them I can produce what my disposition chooses. Whether I have a distressful time or a joyful time depends on what I do in between the limits of the durations.SHH

Whenever we put theology or a plan of salvation or any line of explanation before a man's personal relationship to God, we depart from the Bible. Religion in the Bible is not faith in the rule of God, but faith in the God Who rules. If we put our faith in a credal exposition of God and our creed goes to the winds, as, for instance, Job's creed went, our faith will go too. The only thing to do is to "hang on" in confidence in God. When we get out of this "shell" we shall find an explanation that will justify our faith in Him. The thing that really sustains is not that we feel happy in God, but that God's joy is our energy.[SHH]

Reflection Questions

Am I more concerned about enforcing the rules in the Bible or enjoying my relationship with God? Do I love God with the same intensity that I love my favorite doctrines?

The Way is not creed, nor church, nor doctrine, but Jesus Christ. God can take any man and put the miracle of His joy into Him, and enable him to manifest it in the actual details of his life.[HSGM]

The man who has satisfied his ambition may suddenly become a miserable tyrant and all his joy will go. Jesus said that He wants His joy to be in us. What joy did Jesus have? He failed apparently in everything He came to do; all His disciples forsook Him, He was crucified, and yet He talked of His joy. The joy of our Lord lay in doing what the Father sent Him to do. His purpose was not to succeed, but to fulfill the design of His coming.SHH

Reflection Questions

How does personal ambition destroy joy? What happens to my joy when I fail to meet my goals? Am I willing to accept that personal failure may be part of God's will for my life?

What is the real design of man's creation? Solomon deals with every possible phase of life, including philosophy, religion, prosperity, integrity. He had been through it all, and his verdict is that it all ends in disaster. That is the sum of it all unless a man sees that his "chief end is to glorify God and enjoy Him for ever." To put things on any other basis will end in disaster.SHH

Solomon deals with the expression of practical life as it is, and he finds it a sorry mess. He says a man does not find his true joy in sacrificing or in sin or in labor. True enjoyment is not in what we do but in our relationships. If a man is true to God, everything between birth and death will work out on the line of joy. If we bank on what we do, whether it is good or bad, we are off the track; the one thing that matters is personal relationship.[SHH]

Reflection Questions

Where have I looked to find joy? What have I tried? What has been my biggest disappointment? What have I learned about people, positions, and possessions?

At the basis of trade and civilized life lie oppression and tyranny. Underneath there is a rivalry that stings and bites, and the kindest man will put his heel on his greatest friend. Whether you are king or subject, says Solomon, you cannot find joy in any system of civilized life, or in trade and commerce. These are not the blind statements of a disappointed man, but statements of facts discerned by the wisest man that ever lived.[SHH]

114

We have been shown how to enjoy life. Now we are told of the days when such enjoyment abates. The sparkle of youth will depart. How fascinatingly beautiful this earth can be to the keen vision of youth. The great poets wrote their abiding poems in their early years. It is God's order that the world should be a bright place for bairns. They have the capacity for entering into such natural joys; and it should not be denied them. There is a richer vision for mature minds who have been "born anew" and seen the Kingdom of God. Milton in his blindness saw rarer beauties than through the opened eyes of his youth.[SHH]

Reflection Questions

How does joy increase as the desire for exhilaration decreases? What beauty am I able to see with my soul that I was never able to see with my eyes?

Lord, Your goodness is beyond comparison. Our mouth is filled with laughter, and our tongue with singing; we praise You for the time when we shall come again with joy.[KGD]

When you are joyful, be joyful; when you are sad, be sad. If God has given you a sweet cup, don't make it bitter; and if He has given you a bitter cup, don't try and make it sweet. One of the last lessons we learn is not to be an amateur providence, who says, "I shall not allow that person to suffer." Through suffering is the only way some of us can learn, and if we are shielded God will ultimately take the one who interferes by the scruff of the neck and remove him. The fingers that caress a child may also hurt its flesh; it is the power of love that makes them hurt.SHH

Reflection Questions

Am I able to accept both joy and sorow as gifts from God? Am I guilty of trying to play God and take away all sadness?

The test of honesty is the way we behave in grief and in joy. When we are rightly related to God we must not pretend things are not as they are. It is difficult not to simulate sorrow or gladness, but when we accept God's purpose for us we know that "all things work together for good."SHH

The great motive and inspiration of service is not that God has saved and sanctified me or healed me. All that is a fact, but the great motive of service is the realization that every bit of my life that is of value I owe to the Redemption. I realize with joy that I cannot live my own life; I am a debtor to Christ, and as such I can only realize the fulfillment of His purposes in my life.[SSIY]

Reflection Questions

What is joyful about realizing I cannot live my own life? If Jesus found joy in surrender, what do I have to look forward to by having Christ live through me?

The joy of Jesus Christ was in the absolute self-surrender and self-sacrifice of Himself to His Father, the joy of doing what the Father sent Him to do, and that is the joy He prays may be in His disciples. It is not a question of trying to work as Jesus did, but of having the personal presence of the Holy Ghost Who works in us the nature of Jesus. One of the consolations of the way is the fathomless joy of the Holy Ghost manifesting itself in us as it did in the Son of God in the days of His flesh.[SSIY]

To have our eyes on successful service is one of the greatest snares to a Christian worker, for it has in it the peril of evading the soul's concentration on Jesus Christ, and instead of being friends of the Bridegroom we become antichrists in our domain, working against Him while we use His weapons; amateur providences with the jargon of Divine providence, and when the Bridegroom does speak we shall not hear His voice. Decreasing till he or she is never thought of again, is the true result of devotion, and John says, That is my joy. Rejoice with divine hilarity over the soul who hears the Bridegroom's voice.[PH]

Reflection Questions

Am I trying to increase my own following or do I find joy in seeing it decrease as people start following Jesus instead? Why would I want followers who belong to Jesus?

Lord, for all who are taxed physically, undertake with Your sustaining. Prevent the exacting of the enemy, and may the joy of the Lord be their strength in a marvelous manner.[KGD]

The Bible talks about drinking wine when we are glad (see Psalm 104:15). This is different from the modern view of drinking when we are in the dumps. Solomon is amazingly keen that a man should enjoy the pleasant things, remembering that that is why they are here. The universe is meant for enjoyment. God gives us all things to enjoy. We argue on the rational line— Don't do this or that because it is wrong. Paul argues in this way: Don't do it, not because it is wrong, but because the man who follows you will stumble if he does it, therefore cut it out, never let him see you do it any more (cf. 1 Corinthians 8:9–13).SHH

Reflection Questions

What keeps me from being convinced that God created the universe for our enjoyment? In what way could my refusal to fully enjoy it be an insult to God?

Solomon's attitude is a safe and sane one. When a man is rightly related to God he has to see that he enjoys his own life and that others do too.SHH

119

The joy that a believer can give to God is the purest pleasure God ever allows a saint, and it is very humiliating to realize how little joy we do give Him. We put our trust in God up to a certain point, then we say, "Now I must do my best." There are times when there is no human best to be done, when the Divine best must be left to work, and God expects those of us who know Him to be confident in His ability and power. We have to learn what these fishermen learned, that the Carpenter of Nazareth knew better than they did how to manage the boat. Is Jesus Christ a Carpenter, or is He God to me? If He is only man, why let Him take the tiller of the boat? Why pray to Him? But if He be God, then be heroic enough to go to the breaking-point and not break in your confidence in Him.[PH]

Reflection Questions

Have I ever considered the idea that I could or should give joy to God? Do I know what brings joy to God? In what ways might I give joy to God?

We cannot tie up the wind, it blows where it lists; neither can we tie up the work of the Holy Spirit. Jesus never comes where we expect Him; if He did, He would not have said "Watch. Be ready." Jesus appears in the most illogical connections, where we least expect Him, and the only way we can keep true to God amid the difficulties of work is to be ready for His surprise visits. We have not to depend on the prayers of other people, not to look for the sympathy of God's children, but to be ready for the Lord. It is this intense reality of expecting Him at every turn that gives life the attitude of child wonder that Jesus wants it to have. When we are rightly related to God, life is full of spontaneous joyful uncertainty and expectancy—we do not know what God is going to do next; and He packs our life with surprises all the time.[SSIY]

Reflection Questions

Do I always expect to find Jesus in the same place, doing the same thing? How could that faulty expectation destroy my joy?
Why do I fear spontaneity?

Our Lord speaks about the joy of finding lost things. To me there is always this appeal: The Lord wants to look through my eyes. The Lord wants to think through my brain. The Lord wants to work through my hands. The Lord wants to live and walk in my body for one purpose—to go after the lost from His standpoint. Am I letting Him walk and live in me?[WG]

Reflection Questions

Do I enjoy finding what is lost? Am I an eager participant in God's plan to seek and to save the lost? How might I be guilty of creating a counterfeit spirituality? Am I promoting any kind of rest other than oneness with Jesus and blameless to God?

Spiritual realities can always be counterfeited. "Rest in the Lord" can be turned into pious "rust" in sentiment. What is all our talk about sanctification going to amount to? It should amount to that rest in God which means a oneness with Him such as Jesus had—not only blameless in God's sight, but a deep joy to Him.[PH]

The feast is just beyond the fight. When you have been through the fight, there is the wondrous joy and triumph of the feast. We learn to thank God for the trial of our faith because it works patience. Precious in the sight of God is faith that has been tried. Tried faith is spendable; it is so much wealth stored up in heaven, and the more we go through the trial of our faith, the wealthier we become in the heavenly regions.[PH]

Reflection Questions

In what ways am I fighting the good fight to remain faithful to God? What comfort have I found in dark and scary places? Why is joy so much more precious after trial and tribulation?

God's purpose is to make us full of joy, but it is joy from God's standpoint, not from ours. Why does God bring thunderclouds and disasters when we want green pastures and still waters? Bit by bit we find, behind the clouds, the Father's feet; behind the lightning, an abiding day that has no night; behind the thunder a still small voice that comforts with a comfort that is unspeakable.[PH]

God wants us to realize His sovereignty. We are apt to tie God up in His own laws and allow Him no free will. We say we know what God will do, and suddenly He upsets all our calculations by working in unprecedented ways; just when we expected He would do a certain thing, He did the opposite. There are unexpected issues in life; unexpected joys when we looked for sorrow, and sorrow when we expected joy, until we learn to say, all my expectations are from God.[PH]

Reflection Questions

Why do I insist on prescribing how God will behave? Why would anyone worship a God who is predictable? What have I learned from the disciples' disappointment about setting expectations for God?

The disciples had three years of marvelous delight and joy, and then they were finished and there was pain in the termination of them. No greater sadness than that of the disciples can be imagined. We have all had the equivalent of those three years, a time of great joy while it lasted.[PH]

"He is not here." These are the saddest words on earth. Think what such words mean to mothers who have lost their sons in war, to wives who have lost their husbands. Yet in this connection they are extraordinarily joyful words, for they are followed by "He is risen." He is not here in the ordinary sense of the word, but He is here as the Risen Lord! If we pour out sympathy upon one who is bereaved, all we do is to make that one more submissive to grief. The unique thing about Jesus is that He comes to sorrowing men as a complete Savior from all sorrow.[PH]

Reflection Questions

Why is it difficult to believe that with God all sadness will end one day in gladness? What does the resurrection teach me about the depths of grief and the heights of joy?

The more complicated the actual conditions are, the more delightfully joyful it is to see God open up His way through.[RTR]

Thank God, the joy of the Lord is an actual experience now, and it goes beyond any conscious experience, because the joy of the Lord takes us into the consciousness of God, and the honor at stake in our body is the honor of God. Have we realized that the Son of God has been formed in us by His wonderful Redemption? This is the glory of the saint here and now—the glory of actual holiness manifested in actual life.[PR]

Reflection Questions

Am I putting on habits that are in keeping with Christ's holiness? In what ways is God being formed in me? Am I willing to become weak to regain childlike joy?

God Almighty became the weakest thing in His own creation, a Baby. The mature saint is just like a little child, absolutely simple and joyful. Go on living the life that God would have you live and you will grow younger instead of older. There is a marvelous rejuvenescence when once you let God have His way. If you are feeling very old, then get born again and do more at it.[PR]

There is a stage in our spiritual experience when we do not see the Guide ahead of us, we do not feel the joy of the Lord, there is no exhilaration, yet we have gone too far to go back. At the first we have the idea that everything apart from Christ is bad; but there is much in our former life that is fascinating, any amount of paganism that is clear and vigorous, virtues that are good morally. But we have to discover they are not stamped with the right lineage, and if we are going to live the life of a saint we must turn these good natural things into the spiritual.[PH]

Reflection Questions

What tempts me to go back to my old way of life to recover the happiness I once had? What joy would I miss by doing this? How can I turn my natural abilities into spiritual virtues?

Lord, I do praise You for the sense of joyful fellowship with You. Give me calmness of mind and keenness of purpose; keep me Yours, undoubtedly and undeflectedly.[KGD]

Peace

Life *in the* SPIRIT

Conscience must be educated at the Cross. Always bring the conscience of others to face the Cross of Christ. Is my life worthy of what Jesus Christ did on the Cross? Are there the elements of ability and power and peace stamped with the almightiness that comes through the Cross? If not, I am not where I should be. The Cross of Christ means that the Spirit of God can empower me almightily.[AUG]

Reflection Questions

Does my peace come from my confidence in what Christ did on the Cross or from what I do for myself? Does my peace come from the Spirit within me or cirumstances outside of me?

"If all God can do for me is to destroy the unity I once had, make me a divided personality, give me light that makes me morally insane with longing to do what I cannot do, I would rather be without His salvation, rather remain happy and peaceful without Him." But if this experience is only a stage toward a life of peace and union with God, it is a different matter.[BE]

The revelation of identification means that we are one with God in His Son, but not by obedience, for obedience is nothing more than the human approach to this mightiest of revelations. We enter into identification by the door of obedience and faith, but the oneness is a revelation. When we do touch God we lose all consciousness of being in conscious touch with Him, we are so absorbed with His peace and power that language cannot convey the assurance of the oneness. The experience of sanctification is simply the entrance into this relationship.[AUG]

Reflection Questions

Am I so absorbed in God's peace and power that I don't need to talk about it, I just live it? In what ways do I attempt to make peace without being one with Christ?

There is a dark line in God's face, but what we do know about Him is so full of peace and joy that we can wait for His interpretation.[DI]

After being born again a man experiences peace, but it is a peace maintained at the point of war. The wrong disposition is no longer in the ascendant, but it is there, and the man knows it is. He is conscious of an alternating experience, sometimes he is in ecstasy, sometimes in the dumps; there is no stability, no real spiritual triumph. To take this as the experience of full salvation is to prove God not justified in the Atonement.[BE]

Reflection Questions

What kind of peace do we gain by force? What does it take to maintain that kind of peace? Why is agreement with God necessary for genuine peace?

To be a believer in Jesus Christ means realizing that what Jesus said to Thomas is true: "I am the way, the truth, and the life." Jesus is not the road we leave behind as we travel, but the Way itself. By believing, we enter into that rest of peace, holiness, and eternal life because we are abiding in Him.[AUG]

When God begins His work in us He does not make a mighty difference in our external lives, but He shifts the center of our confidence. Instead of relying on ourselves and other people, we rely on God, and are kept in perfect peace. We all know the difference it makes if we have someone who believes in us and in whom we believe. There is no possibility of being crushed. The Great Life is not that we believe for something, but that when we are up against things in circumstances or in our own disposition, we stake our all on Jesus Christ's honor.[AUG]

Reflection Questions

How does my position in Christ keep me from being crushed by conflict? How does God's peace allow me to be perfected through suffering?

May the God of peace sanctify us wholly so that we are no longer sickly souls retarding His purposes, but perfected through suffering.[GW]

The devil is the adversary of God in the rule of man and Satan is his representative. Because a thing is satanic does not mean that it is abominable and immoral. As our Lord said, "that which is highly esteemed among men is abomination in the sight of God" (Luke 16:15). Satan rules this world under the inspiration of the devil and men are peaceful: "when a strong man armed keeps his palace, his goods are in peace," there is no breaking out into sin and wrongdoing. One of the most cunning travesties is to represent Satan as the instigator of external sins. The satanically-managed man is moral, upright, proud and individual; he is absolutely self-governed and has no need of God.[BFB]

Reflection Questions

Behind what good things does Satan hide?
How does Satan keep peace? What lies does he tell to control those who are weary of war?

Lord, may I be full of the calm peace which comes from knowing that You reign.[KGD]

The preacher is there not by right of his personality or oratorical powers, but by right of the message he proclaims. Who is the man that attracts us today? The man with a striking personality and we don't care about his message. The New Testament preacher has to move men to do what they are dead-set against doing—giving up the right to themselves to Jesus Christ; consequently the preaching of the Gospel awakens a terrific longing, but an equally intense resentment. The aspect of the Gospel that awakens desire in a man is the message of peace and goodwill—but I must give up my right to myself to get there.[BE]

Reflection Questions

Why am I so often more moved by the messenger than the message? What longing does the messenger ignite? What resentment does the message fuel? How can I make peace with these war-prone emotions?

O Lord, I do thank You for the relief and inspiration that has flowed into me and visited my inner kingdom. Fill me now with Your calm peace.[KGD]

For a man to be undisturbed and in unity with himself is a good condition, not a bad one, because a united personality means freedom from self-consciousness; but if his peace is without any consideration of Jesus Christ it is simply the outcome of this disposition of darkness which keeps men alienated from the life of God. When Jesus Christ comes in He upsets this false unity.ᴮᴱ

Reflection Questions

Does my sense of peace come from my unity
with Christ or my compromise with Satan?
What is the danger of peace apart from Christ?

If I was peaceful and happy, living a clean upright life, why should Jesus Christ come with a standard of holiness I never dreamt of? Simply because that peace was the peace of death, a peace altogether apart from God. The coming of Jesus Christ to the natural man means the destruction of all peace that is not based on a personal relationship to Himself.ᴮᴱ

Jesus Christ's one aim is to bring us back into peace and oneness with God. The whole purpose of the Redemption is to give back to man the original source of life. In a regenerated man this means "Christ . . . formed in you." Am I willing that the old disposition should be crucified with Christ? If I am, Jesus Christ will take possession of me and will baptize me into His life until I bear a family likeness to Him. It is a lonely path, a path of death, but it means ultimately being at peace with Divinity. The Christian life does not take its pattern from good men, but from God Himself.[BE]

Reflection Questions

What is the difference between peace with other people and peace with God? In what ways can peace with people give me the faulty assurance that I am at peace with God?

If you allow anything to hide the face of Jesus Christ from you, you are either disturbed or you have a false security. The peace of God comes from looking into the face of Jesus and realizing His undisturbedness.[RTR]

We must be like a plague of mosquitoes to the Almighty with our fussy little worries and anxieties, and the perplexities we imagine, all because we won't get into the elemental life with God which Jesus came to give. "His love in times past" should enable us to rest confidentially in Him. There is security from yesterday, security for tomorrow, and security for today. It was this knowledge that gave our Lord the imperturbable peace He always had.[BE]

Reflection Questions

What worries and anxieties do I indulge in that reveal my lack of peace? What societies and systems do we build to minimize our need for peace with God?

Communities are man's attempt at building up the city of God; man is confident that if only God will give him time enough he will build not only a holy city, but a holy community and establish peace on earth, and God is allowing him ample opportunity to try, until he is satisfied that God's way is the only way.[HG]

Man was turned out into destitution, and was thus divided from Deity; God disappeared from him, and he disappeared from God. There are three false unities possible in a man's experience—sensuality, drunkenness, and the devil—whereby man's spirit, soul, and body are brought into harmony and he is quite peaceful, quite happy, with no sense of death about him. A drunken man has no self-consciousness, he is perfectly delivered from all the things which disintegrate and upset. Sensuality and Satan will do the same; but each of these unities is only possible for a time.[BP]

Reflection Questions

What false peace is my biggest temptation?
What imposter do I allow to mimic God? What vice provides me a few moments of peace?
Why do I settle for so little?

If we are to be sanctified, it must be by the God of peace Himself. The power that makes the life of the saint does not come from our efforts at all, it comes from the heart of the God of peace.[IYSA]

We preach to men as if they were conscious of being dying sinners, but they are not. They are having a good time, and all our talk about the need to be born again is from a domain they know nothing about; because some men try to drown unhappiness in worldly pleasures it does not follow all are like that. There is nothing attractive about the Gospel to the natural man; the only man who finds the Gospel attractive is the man who is convicted of sin. Apart from a knowledge of Jesus Christ, and apart from being crumpled up by conviction of sin, men have a disposition which keeps them perfectly happy and peaceful. Conviction of sin is produced by the incoming of the Holy Spirit because conscience is promptly made to look at God's demands.[BE]

Reflection Questions

What message of peace do I have for those who don't know they are alienated from God? Why is the gospel not attractive to those who love life the way it is? How does God's goodness keep me from realizing my need for Him?

Satan is never represented in the Bible as being guilty of doing wrong things: he is a wrong being. Men are responsible for doing wrong things, and they do wrong things because of the wrong disposition in them. The moral cunning of our nature makes us blame Satan when we know perfectly well we should blame ourselves; the true blame for sins lies in the wrong disposition in us. In all probability Satan is as much upset as the Holy Ghost is when men fall in external sin, but for a different reason. When men go into external sin and upset their lives, Satan knows perfectly well that they will want another Ruler, a Savior and Deliverer; as long as Satan can keep men in peace and unity and harmony apart from God, he will do so (see Luke 11:21–22).[BP]

Reflection Questions

Who do I blame for my sin? What does Satan gain if I lead an upright and moral life? What does he lose if I mess up so badly that I recognize my need for peace apart from my own efforts?

When Satan rules, men's souls are in peace, they are not troubled or upset like other men, but quite happy and peaceful. There is only one right at-one-ment, and that is in Jesus Christ; only one right unity, and that is when body, soul and spirit are united to God by the Holy Ghost through the marvellous Atonement of the Lord Jesus Christ.[BP]

Reflection Questions

Are my body, soul, and spirit all united in Christ or still in conflict with each other?

Is my sense of peace dependent on getting what I want or receiving what I need?

The gospel of Jesus Christ does not present what men want, it presents exactly what they need. As long as you talk about being happy and peaceful, men like to listen to you; but talk about having the disposition of the soul altered, and that the garden of the soul has first of all to be turned into a wilderness and afterwards into a garden of the Lord, and you will find opposition right away.[BP]

A darkened heart is a terrible thing, because a darkened heart may make a man peaceful. A man says—"My heart is not bad, I am not convicted of sin; all this talk about being born again and filled with the Holy Spirit is so much absurdity." The natural heart needs the Gospel of Jesus, but it does not want it, it will fight against it, and it takes the convicting Spirit of God to make men and women know they need to experience a radical work of grace in their hearts.[BP]

Reflection Questions

What kind of peace do I have: the kind that comes from confessing who I am and being reconciled to God or from ignoring who I am and living in denial?

There are times when inner peace is based on ignorance; but when we awake to the troubles of life, which more than ever before surge and heave in threatening billows, inner peace is impossible unless it is received from our Lord. When our Lord spoke peace, He made peace. Have you ever received what He spoke?[CD]

When Satan, the prince of this world, guards this world, his goods—the souls of men—are in peace; they are quite happy, hilarious and full of life. One of the most misleading statements is that worldlings have not a happy time; they have a thoroughly happy time. The point is that their happiness is on the wrong level, and when they come across Jesus Christ, Who is the enemy of all that happiness, they experience annoyance. People must be persuaded that Jesus Christ has a higher type of life for them, otherwise they feel they had better not have come across Him. When a worldly person who is happy, moral and upright comes in contact with Jesus Christ, Who came to destroy all that happiness and peace and put it on a different level, he has to be persuaded that Jesus Christ is a Being worthy to do this, and instead of the Gospel being attractive at first, it is the opposite.[BP]

Reflection Questions

What faulty beliefs do I have about peace?
What makes the peace of God superior
to the peace of the world?

The first sign of the dethronement of God is the apparent absence of the devil and the peaceful propaganda that is spread abroad. The great cry today is "Be broad; accommodate yourself with evil so diplomatically that the line of demarcation is gone. Run up the white flag, say to the prince of this world, "We have been too puritanical in the past, there has been too clear a division between us, now we will go arm-in-arm." Is that the order? Never! Satan is the prince of this world, and during this dispensation he has power to give authority to those who will yield to him and compromise. We are here to stand true to God, not to attack men. The messenger of God has to stand where Jesus Christ stood, steadfast in obedience to God first.[BSG]

Reflection Questions

What peaceful propaganda do I believe? What does Satan want me to believe about peace? In what way do I accommodate evil to maintain peace?

The source of peace is God, not myself; it never is my peace but always His, and if once He withdraws, it is not there. If I allow anything to hide the face, the countenance, the memory, the consideration of our Lord Jesus from me, then I am either disturbed or I have a false security.[CD]

Reflection Questions

What happens when I try to manufacture peace from within? What do I allow to come between myself and God? What false sense of security do I need to guard against? What little things crowd into my life and mar the beauty of God's peace?

Lord, in my consciousness this morning a crowd of little things presses in and I bring them straight to Your presence. In Your wisdom, say, "Peace, be still!" and may my ordered life confess the beauty of Your peace.[KGD]

When God became Incarnate in Jesus Christ for the purpose of removing sin, men saw nothing in Him to desire. But when the heart of a sinner is reached, that is a state of heart and mind able to understand why it was necessary for God to become Incarnate. The worst state a man could be in is never to have had a twinge of conviction of sin, everything happy and peaceful, but absolutely dead to the realm of things Jesus represents.[BSG]

Reflection Questions

Why is misplaced peace so deadly? Why is easy peace so temporary? Why is comfort the enemy of peace?

The majority of us are shallow, we do not bother our heads about Reality. We are taken up with actual comforts, with actual ease and peace, and when the Spirit of God comes in and disturbs the equilibrium of our life we prefer to ignore what He reveals.[PR]

The idea of peace in connection with personality is that every power is in perfect working order to the limit of activity. That is what Jesus means when He says "My peace." Never have in mind the idea of jadedness or stagnation in connection with peace. Health is physical peace, but health is not stagnation; health is the perfection of physical activity. Virtue is moral peace, but virtue is not innocence; virtue is the perfection of moral activity. Holiness is spiritual peace, but holiness is not quietness; holiness is the intensest spiritual activity.[BSG]

Reflection Questions

In what ways does inactivity give a false sense of peace? Why is activity required for peace? Why does self-interest have to part in peace?

The profound realization of God makes you too unspeakably peaceful to be capable of any self-interest.[NKW]

Jesus had joy and peace to the last reach of His personality. With us it is possible to have joy and peace in one domain and disturbance and unrest in another; we have spells of joy and spells that are the opposite of joy, tribulation that brings distress; but there is a time coming when there will be no more tribulation, no more distress, when every part of our personality will be as full of joy and peace as was the founder of our faith.[BSG]

Reflection Questions

What must happen before peace can prevail? What must happen to my worry and discontent? How can I expect to have peace if I insist on having everything my way?

When I wish I was somewhere else I am not doing my duty to God where I am. I have no right to say I am content and yet have a mood that is not contented. If I am set on some change of circumstances, I have worried myself outside the moral frontier where He works and my soul won't sing. There is no joy in God, no peace in believing.[HG]

We limit ourselves and our conceptions of God by ignoring the side of the Divine Nature best symbolized by womanhood, and the Comforter surely represents this side of the Divine Nature. It is the Comforter Who sheds abroad the love of God in our hearts. It is the Comforter Who baptizes us into oneness with Jesus, in the amazing language of Scripture, until we are indwelt by a mysterious union with God. It is the Comforter Who brings forth the fruit of love, joy, peace, long-suffering, kindness, goodness, faithfulness, meekness, temperance. Guidance by His sympathy leads by a blessed discipline into an understanding of God which passes knowledge.[CD]

Reflection Questions

Why is it impossible to have peace with God if we are in conflict with the opposite gender? Why does peace require tenderness as well as power, purity as well as compassion?

O Lord, remove this bondage of thought, and bring peace and purity and power. Fill me this day with Your tenderness and compassion and grace.[KGD]

When by the discipline of His Divine guidance, we know Him, and He going with us gives us Rest, then Time and Eternity are merged and lost in that amazing vital relationship. The union is one not of mystic contemplation, but of intense perfection of activity, not the Rest of the placid peace of stagnation, but the Rest of perfect motion.[CD]

Reflection Questions

How is the "rest of perfect motion" different from the "peace of stagnation"? In what ways is social and political peace the enemy of peace with God?

The human soul is so mysterious that in the moment of a great tragedy men get face to face with things they never gave heed to before. In times of peace, how many of us bother one iota about the state of men's hearts toward God? Yet these are the things that produce pain in the heart of God, not the wars and the devastation that so upset us. [CD]

Let us stop all futile wailings that express themselves in such statements as "War ought not to be." War is, and we must not waste our time or our Lord's by giving way to any surfeit of screaming invective for or against any one or any thing. Let us face life as it is, not as we feel it ought to be, for it never will be what it ought to be until the kingdom of this world is become the kingdom of our Lord, and of His Christ. The seemliness of Christian conduct is not consistent adherence to a mere principle of peace, but standing true to Jesus Christ.[CD]

Reflection Questions

How can there be peace in the world as long as there is conflict between Christians? How can non-Christians make peace if Christians cannot?

It is an easy business to preach peace when you are in health and have everything you want, but the Bible preaches peace when things are in a howling tumult of passion and sin and iniquity; it is in the midst of anguish and terror that we realize who God is and the marvel of what He can do.[NI]

Jerusalem and Jesus! What a contrast! With what an amazed stare of contempt the personal powers of Jerusalem confronted Jesus, the despised and rejected! Yet He was their Peace for time and eternity, and the things that belonged to their peace were all connected with Him. He said to His disciples: "These things have I spoken unto you, that in Me you may have peace. In the world you have tribulation: but be of good cheer: I have overcome the world" (John 16:33).CD

Reflection Questions

In what ways do I despise the peace that Jesus wants to give me? In what areas do I refuse to overcome the world? What road to peace am I unwilling to travel?

Our Lord is not a road we leave behind us, He is the Way to the Father in which we abide (John 15:4). The Way to the Father is not by the law, nor by obedience, or creed, but Jesus Christ Himself, He is the Way of the Father whereby any and every soul may be in peace, in joy, and in divine courage.CD

The peace of sins forgiven, the peace of a conscience at rest with God, is not the peace that Jesus imparts. Those are the immediate results of believing and obeying Him, but it is His own peace He gives, and He never had any sins to be forgiven or an outraged conscience to appease. Have you ever received His peace? When you are right with God, receive your peace by studying in consecrated concentration our Lord Himself; it is the peace that comes from looking at His face and remembering the undisturbed condition of our Lord in every set of circumstances.^{CD}

Reflection Questions

In what ways does my peace with God extend to my relationships and my circumstances? What do others learn about the peace of God by observing me?

Nothing else is in the least like His peace. It is the peace of God, which passes all understanding. Are you looking unto Jesus just now in the immediate pressing matter and receiving from Him peace? Then He will be a gracious benediction of peace in and through you.^{CD}

Reflected peace is the greatest evidence that I am right with God, for I am at liberty to turn my mind to Him. If I am not right with God I can never turn my mind anywhere but on myself. Are you painfully disturbed just now, distracted by the waves and billows of God's providential permission? Having turned over, as it were, the boulders of your belief, do you still find no well of peace or joy or comfort — all is barren? Then look up and receive the undisturbedness of our Lord Jesus Christ. Above and in the facts of war and pain and difficulties He reigns, peaceful.[CD]

Reflection Questions

What do selfish thoughts tell me about my concept of peace? What anxious thoughts do I need to clear from my mind before I can have peace with God and others?

Before the Spirit of God can bring peace of mind He has to clear out the rubbish, and before He can do that He has to give us an idea of what rubbish there is.[SHL]

The world means what it says, but it cannot impart. Our Lord imparts what He says. He does not give like the world does. Jesus Christ imparts the Holy Spirit to me, and the Holy Spirit sheds abroad the love of God in my heart. The peace of Jesus is not a cherished piece of property that I possess; it is a direct impartation from Him, and my enjoying His peace depends on my recognizing this.^{CD}

Reflection Questions

What happens when I try to possess peace? What is the difference between something I possess and something that is part of me? What trivial distractions still trouble me? Why?

This kind of peace banishes trouble just now and presently. Our Lord says in effect, "Don't let your heart be troubled out of its relationship with Me." It is never the big things that disturb us, but the trivial things. Do I believe that the circumstances bothering me just now do not perplex Jesus Christ at all? If I do, His peace is mine. If I try to worry it out, I obliterate Him and deserve what I get.^{CD}

When we confer with Jesus Christ over other lives all the perplexity goes, because He has no perplexity, and our concern is to abide in Him. Let us be confident in His wisdom and His certainty that all will be well. "He abideth faithful; for He cannot deny Himself" (2 Tim. 2:13). The angels' song is still the truth: "Glory to God in high heaven, and peace on earth for men whom He favors."[CD]

Reflection Questions

What perplexities disturb my peace? What gestures of peace do I expect from others that I am unwilling to extend? In what ways must I yet conform to the pleasure of God?

The way of inward peace is in all things to be conformed to the pleasure and disposition of the divine will. Such as would have all things succeed and come to pass according to their own fancy, are not come to know this way, and therefore lead a harsh and bitter life, always restless or out of humor, without treading in the way of peace which consists in a total conformity to the will of God.[CD]

When the Holy Spirit begins to try and break into the house of our possessions in order to grant us the real life of God, we look on Him as a robber, as a disturber of our peace, because when He comes He reveals the things which are not of God and must go; and they are the things which constituted our life before He came in, our golden affections were carefully nested in them. The thing that hurts shows where we live.[GW]

Reflection Questions

In what ways could my lack of peace be due to the work God is doing in my life to convict me of sin? In what ways could the presence of peace be due to the work of Satan trying to convince me that everything I am doing is okay?

No man is ever the same after listening to the truth. He may say he pays no attention to it, he may appear to forget all about it, but at any moment the truth may spring up into his consciousness and destroy all his peace of mind.[DI]

Epochs and civilizations appear after a time to be flung on the scrap-heap by God in a strangely careless manner. The remarkable thing in the record of the Ages is that each Age ends in apparent disaster. The saint knows that God reigns, and that the clouds are but the dust of his Father's feet and he has no need to fear. He feels assured that these catastrophic occurrences are but incidental, and that a higher peace and a purer character are to be the permanent result. History is fulfilling prophecy all the time.[GW]

Reflection Questions

What does the downfall of dictators indicate about the effectiveness of peace that is imposed on people? What does history teach me about human attempts to make peace?

The path of peace for us is to hand ourselves over to God and ask Him to search us, not what we think we are, or what other people think we are, or what we persuade ourselves we are or would like to be, but, "Search me out, O God, explore me as I really am in Thy sight."[BP]

Jesus is the "Prince of Peace" because only in Him can men have God's good-will and peace on earth. Thank God, through that beloved Son the great peace of God may come to every heart and to every nation under heaven, but it can come in no other way. None of us can ever have good-will toward God if we won't listen to His Son. The only way to peace and salvation and power, and to all that God has in the way of benedictions and blessings for us individually and for the whole world, is in the Son of Man.[HSGM]

Reflection Questions

In what ways do I try to make peace with God without going through His Son? Is my peace passionate or lethargic?

When the phrase "the Passion of our Lord" is used it means the transfiguration of peace and power and patience.[HSGM]

Jesus Christ bases all His teaching on the fundamental fact that God can do for a man what he cannot do for himself. It is an easy business to say I love my enemies when I haven't any, but when I have an enemy, when a man has done me or those who belong to me, a desperate wrong, what is my attitude as a Christian to be? What we are up against just now is the danger of not making the basis of forgiveness and peace the right kind. If it is not the basis of perfect justice, it will fail. We may succeed in calling a truce, but that is not peace, and before long we will be at it again.[HSGM]

Reflection Questions

What is the difference between a truce and peace? What does peace have that a truce does not?

When we are rightly related to God as Jesus was, the spiritual life becomes as natural as the life of a child. The one dominant note of the life after sanctification is the simplicity of a child, full of the radiant peace and joy of God.[BSG]

Satisfaction is too often the peace of death; wonder is the very essence of life. Beware of losing the wonder. The the first thing that stops wonder is religious conviction. Whenever you give a trite testimony the wonder is gone. The only evidence of salvation or sanctification is that the sense of wonder is developing, not at things as they are, but at the One who made them as they are.[HSGM]

Reflection Questions

Have I sacrificed peace for satisfaction? Have I given up on wonder for the sake of serenity? Would I rather have peaceful circumstances or a peace that can survive turbulent circumstances?

The peace of this world can never be the peace of God. The peace of physical health, of mental healthy-mindedness, of prosperous circumstances, of civilization—not one of these is the peace of God, but the outcome of the souls of men being garrisoned by the prince of this world (see Luke 11:21).[HG]

162

We are apt to make salvation mean the saving of our skin. The death of our body, the sudden breaking-up of the house of life, may be the salvation of our soul. In times of peace "honesty may be the best policy," but if we work on the idea that it is better physically and prosperously to be good, that is the wrong motive; the right motive is devotion to God, remaining absolutely true to God, no matter what it costs.[HG]

Reflection Questions

Am I willing to remain true to God even if it results in loss of peace? Have I settled for a form of peace that is more like death than life? Would I rather be satisfied with myself or at peace with God?

The thing we kick against most is the question of pain and suffering. We have naturally the idea that if we are happy and peaceful we are all right. Happiness is not a sign that we are right with God; happiness is a sign of satisfaction, that is all, and the majority of us can be satisfied on too low a level. Jesus Christ disturbs every kind of satisfaction that is less than delight in God.[ITWBP]

God's love is wrath toward wrong; He is never tender to that which hates goodness. The Bible reveals that once communion with God is severed, the basis of life is chaos and wrath. The chaotic elements may not show themselves at once, but they will presently. All that this Book says about corruption in connection with the flesh is as certain as God is on His throne if the life is not rightly related to God. When we speak of the wrath of God we must not picture Him as an angry judge on the throne of heaven, bringing a lash about people when they do what He does not want. There is no element of personal vindictiveness in God. It is rather that God's constitution of things is such that when a man becomes severed from God his life tumbles into turmoil and confusion, into agony and distress, it is hell at once, and he will never get out of it unless he turns to God; immediately he turns, chaos is turned into cosmos, wrath into love, distress into peace.[CHI]

Reflection Questions

In what ways do I try to gain peace without giving up sin? If God is sinless, how can He make peace with sinners?

Often when a problem or perplexity harasses the mind and there seems no solution, after a night's rest you find the solution easy, and the problem has no further perplexity. Think of the security of the saint in sleeping or in waking, "Thou shalt not be afraid for the terror by night, nor for the arrow that flies by day." Sleep is God's celestial nurse. God deals with the unconscious life of the soul in places where only He and His angels have charge. As you retire to rest, give your soul and God a time together, and commit your life to God with a conscious peace for the hours of sleep, and deep and profound developments will go on in spirit, soul and body by the kind creating hand of our God.[HG]

Reflection Questions

Do I keep God from ministering to me by refusing to rest? Do I think that the work I do for God while awake is more important than the work God does while I sleep? How will I ever have peace if I refuse to rest?

The peace of Christ is synonymous with His very nature, and the working of that peace was exhibited in Our Lord's earthly life. It is the God of peace Who sanctifies wholly. The gift of the peace of Christ on the inside; the garrison of God on the outside, then I have to see that I allow the peace of God to regulate all that I do, that is where my responsibility comes in—"let the peace of Christ rule in your hearts."[HG]

Reflection Questions

What does it mean to allow peace to rule my heart? What is the difference between staying calm and living in peace? What is the difference between calmness and peace?

One of the things which we need to be cured of by the God of peace is the petulant struggle of doing things for ourselves. Has the God of peace brought you into a calm, or is there a clamor and a struggle still? Are you still hanging on to some obstinate conviction of your own?—still struggling with some particular line of things you want.[IYSA]

What kind of shoes do you wear? How many can say of us, "As soon as I heard your step I felt better"? Or do they say, "It was when your step came into my life that all went wrong; it was when the step of your friendship began with me that I began to lose out with God"? Put on the armour of God, keep the heart right with God, and wherever you go, you will shed the preparation of the gospel of peace. Wherever the saint goes there is the shedding of the benediction of the blessing of God, or there is the coming of the conviction of the Spirit of God.[IYSA]

Reflection Questions

Do people expect war or peace when I enter the room? Do I sometimes leave home without the gospel of peace? Am I at peace with God about everything He is doing in my life?

When once you let the God of peace grip you by salvation and squeeze the suspicion out of you till you are quiet before Him, the believing attitude is born, there is no more suspicion, you are in moral agreement with God about everything He wants to do.[IYSA]

How much of faith, hope, and love is worked in us when we try to convince somebody else? It is not our business to convince other people, that is the insistence of a merely intellectual, unspiritual life. The Spirit of God will do the convicting when we are in the relationship where we simply convey God's word. We exploit the word of God in order to fit it into some view of our own that we have generated; but when it comes to the great calm peace and rest of the Lord Jesus, we can easily test where we are. To "rest in the Lord" is the perfection of inward activity. In the ordinary reasoning of man it means sitting with folded arms and letting God do everything; in reality it is being so absolutely stayed on God that we are free to do the active work of men without fuss. The times God works most wonderfully are the times we never think about it.ITWBP

Reflection Questions

How much of my unrest comes from trying to create peace on my terms rather than God's? Which part of the peace-making process belongs to God and which to me?

The attitude to sickness in the Bible is totally different from the attitude of people who believe in faith-healing. The Bible's attitude is not that God sends sickness or that sickness is of the devil, but that sickness is a fact usable by both God and the devil. God's Book deals with facts. Health and sickness are facts, not fancies. There are cases recorded in the Bible, and in our own day, of people who have been marvelously healed, for what purpose? For us to imitate them? Never, but in order that we might discern what lies behind the individual relationship to a personal God. The peace arising from fact is unintelligent and dangerous. People who base on the fact of health are at peace, but it is often a peace which makes them callous. On the other hand, people who accept the fact of being sick are inclined to have a jaundiced eye for everything healthy. For a man to make health his god is to put himself merely at the head of the brute creation.[PS]

Reflection Questions

Is my peace based on hard cold facts or on the confident assurance that God will use all things to further His kingdom?

It is a mistake to say that because prayer brings us peace and joy and makes us feel better, therefore it is a Divine thing. This is the mere accident or effect of prayer, there is no real God-given revelation in it. This is the God-given revelation: that when we are born again of the Spirit of God and indwelt by the Holy Spirit, He intercedes for us with a tenderness and an understanding akin to the Lord Jesus Christ and akin to God, that is, He expresses the unutterable for us.[IYSA]

Reflection Questions

If Jesus is interceding on my behalf, what could be causing turbulence in my spirit? If Jesus is praying for me to have peace, what am I doing to keep His prayer from being answered?

The great mighty power of the God of peace is slipped into the soul under the call for supreme sanctification. Some of us are far too turbulent in spirit to experience even the first glimpse of what sanctification means.[IYSA]

The kingdoms of this world have become intensely individualistic, with no love for God, or care for one another. The insistence of nations is that they must keep the national peace—in the way they have been doing it! In the whirlwind of nations, many men have lost—not their faith in God (I never met a man who lost his faith in God), but their belief in their beliefs, and for a while they think they have lost their faith in God. They have lost the conception which has been presented to them as God, and are coming to God on a new line.LG

Reflection Questions

How much of my security and peace is the outcome of the civilized life we live? How much of it is built on my faith in God?

Thousands of people are happy without God in this world, but that kind of happiness and peace is on a wrong level. Jesus Christ came to send a sword through every peace that is not based on a personal relationship to Himself. RTR

171

There is one thing worse than war and that is sin, the thing that startles us is not the thing that startles God. We are scared and terrorized when our social order is broken, and well we may be, but how many of us in times of peace and civilization bother one iota about the state of men's hearts toward God? Yet that is the thing that produces pain in the heart of God, not the wars and devastations that so upset us.[LG]

Reflection Questions

What is sin if not war against God? Why are we more concerned about social and political upheaval than we are about those who establish their own moral code in opposition to God?

The carnal mind is the result of the Spirit of God being in a man but who has not quite yielded to Him. Instead of the Spirit of God bringing peace and joy and delight, His incoming has brought disturbance. The natural pagan who is a moral and upright man is more delightful to meet than the Christian who has enough of the Spirit of God to spoil his sin but not enough to deliver him from it.[PH]

It is an easy business to preach, an appallingly easy thing to tell other people what to do; it is another thing to have God's message turned into a boomerang— "You have been teaching these people that they should be full of peace and of joy, but what about yourself? Are you full of peace and joy?" The truthful witness is the one who lets his light shine in works which exhibit the disposition of Jesus; one who lives the truth as well as preaches it.[LG]

Reflection Questions

What truth do I preach better than I practice? Is there unresolved conflict between me and someone else that is like a shade pulled over the light of Christ in me? What pride keeps me from making peace?

The way God's life manifests itself in joy is in a peace which has no desire for praise. When a man delivers a message which he knows is the message of God, the witness to the fulfilment of the created purpose is given instantly, the peace of God settles down, and the man cares for neither praise nor blame from anyone.[LG]

In our spiritual life God does not provide pinnacles on which we stand like spiritual acrobats; He provides tablelands of easy and delightful security. Recall the conception you had of holiness before you stood by the grace of God where you do today. It was the conception of a breathless standing on a pinnacle for a second at a time, but never with the thought of being able to live there. But when the Holy Spirit brought you there, you found it was not a pinnacle, but a plateau, a broad way, where the provision of strength and peace comes all the time.[MFL]

Reflection Questions

Am I living in anticipation of some spiritual "high" and not enjoying the peaceful plateau? Are my faulty expectations of the spiritual life causing conflict in the family of God?

If we are sanctified by the power of the God of peace, our self life is blameless before Him, there is nothing to hide; and the more we bring our soul under the search-light of God the more we realize the ineffable comfort of the supernatural work He has done.[LG]

We talk about "circumstances over which we have no control." None of us have control over our circumstances, but we are responsible for the way we pilot ourselves in the midst of things as they are. Two boats can sail in opposite directions in the same wind, according to the skill of the pilot. The pilot who conducts his vessel on to the rocks says he could not help it, the wind was in that direction; the one who took his vessel into the harbour had the same wind, but he knew how to trim his sails so that the wind conducted him in the direction he wanted. The power of the peace of God will enable you to steer your course in the mix-up of ordinary life.[MFL]

Reflection Questions

What power does peace have in my life? Do I rob peace of its power by insisting that it submit to my "common sense"? What could be more secure than being at peace with a loving God?

O Lord, unto You do I turn, unto You. I am but a homeless waif until You touch me with the security of Your peace, the sweet sense of Your love.[KGD]

Re-examine for yourself the teaching in the Bible which you say you don't understand, and see if the reason is not your dislike of what is taught. The destruction and terrors of God's punishment are as much God's decree as are the peace and joy and prosperity of God. Damnation and salvation are not natural results, they are Divine results. We can choose the way we take, but we have no control over where that way ends.[NE]

Reflection Questions

How many of my questions about the Bible have to do with not wanting to believe what it says? How much of the conflict in my life has to do with not wanting to make peace?

Immediately Jesus Christ comes in that peace is gone, and instead there is the sword of conviction. A man does not need the Holy Spirit to tell him that external sins are wrong, ordinary culture and education will do that; but it does take the Holy Spirit to convict us of sin as our Lord defined it. If once we have allowed Jesus Christ to upset the equilibrium, holiness is the inevitable result, or no peace for ever.[SHL]

176

The love of God cannot make room for sin or self-interest, therefore the appeal of the love of God is not that of kindness and gentleness, but of holiness. If God were love according to our natural view of love He ought never to cause us pain, He ought to allow us to be peaceful; but the first thing God does is to cause us pain and to rouse us wide awake. He comes into our lives all along with ideals and truths which annoy and sting us and break up our rest, until He brings us to the one point, that it is only moral and spiritual relationships which last. That is why God looks cruel judged from the human sentimental standpoint; He loves us so much that He will not prevent us being hurt.[NI]

Reflection Questions

In what realms will God not allow me to be at peace? What ideals does He have for me that seem unreasonable? What beauty is He creating in me?

O Lord, I do thank You for the condition of heart and motive that Your grace has wrought in me. But when in my actual life shall I express before the world the beauty of Your peace?[KGD]

The majority of people do not see what is wrong, and the talk of a prophet like Jeremiah is nonsense. We never can face the things that are wrong, apart from God, without getting insane. If sin is a trifling thing and we can preach to the healing of people and bring peace on any other line, then the tragedy of the Cross is a huge blunder. To live a life hid with Christ in God means we see at times what men and women are like without God, from God's standpoint, and it also means vicarious intercession for them, while they look upon us with pity.[NJ]

Reflection Questions

Why must we be clear about what is wrong before we can be made right? Why is it impossible to make peace where sin is present? Why is purity required for peace?

Clear from me my hidden faults. Keep Your servant also from presumptuous sins. Oh that I could find You exhibiting in me Your peace and purity![KGD]

If a man or woman has known God and turned back, then the corresponding riot of calamity is in proportion; that is why comparing ourselves with ourselves, we do always err from the truth. The one relationship to maintain is the simple one toward God. Keeping that, it is life and peace and joy; outside that, it is terror and anguish wherever you may be found. The measure of my misery when I turn from God is proportioned to my knowledge of Him when I walked with Him.[NJ]

Reflection Questions

How does my relationship with God affect my ability to live in peace with others? Why are peace and prosperity not a reliable measure of our standing with God?

The idea is that if we are in joy and peace we are all right. Standing in the courts of the temple Jeremiah is talking to a people battened in prosperity, but the prophet hears what is coming. Just before the judgment of God the majority of people are happy; they are infatuated. [NJ]

When God seems to let calamity fall on a good person, it leads to the salvation of a bad person. This is difficult to put in words. Correction is not for the detection of faults, but in order to make perfect. Those who take God's way of coming into the light will find ultimately nothing but unspeakable joy and peace, life and love.ᴺᴶ

Reflection Questions

How might God be using calamity in my life for the good of someone else? How does God use restlessness to make me aware of my sinfulness? Why is truth essential for peace?

We are here for one purpose—to stand for the revelation of God's truth to the people of God and to sinners. The tendency is to water down God's truth in the case of some darling relationship and say God did not mean what we know He did. We must never shield a person from God's truth; if we do, we put them into the dark and deepen their torture instead of their peace.ᴺᴶ

God makes His Word living by speaking it to you. There is a feeling of deep settled peace when the Holy Ghost brings a word, full of light and illumination. Never cling to the Word of God in an experience as something separable from God. If you do, the result will be perplexity arising out of a false confidence not rooted in God. Beware of the obstinacy of belief in a word God spoke once your connection with Him is severed. You never find a noble, pure character obstinate. Every trace of obstinacy means sensual selfishness somewhere; it is not strength of will, but lack of will.ᴺᴶ

Reflection Questions

Am I able to discern genuine peace from false confidence? Am I willing to listen to people who tell me I am being obstinate? Am I willing to accept trouble as a stepping stone to peace?

As we go on in life and grow in grace, we realize more and more wonderingly what the peace of Jesus means. Paul says, tribulation, turmoil, trouble, afflictions all around everywhere, yet the peace of Jesus manifests itself, and the life grows as the lily spiritually.ᴼᴮᴴ

We talk about the peace of Jesus, but have we ever realized what that peace was like? Read the story of His life, the thirty years of quiet submission at Nazareth, the three years of service, the slander and spite, back-biting and hatred He endured, all unfathomably worse than anything we shall ever have to go through; and His peace was undisturbed, it could not be violated. It is that peace that God will exhibit in us in the heavenly places; not a peace like it, but that peace. In all the rush of life, in working for our living, in all conditions of bodily life, wherever God engineers our circumstances—"My peace"—the imperturbable, inviolable peace of Jesus imparted to us in every detail of our lives.OBH

Reflection Questions

Do I have the kind of peace that can withstand the assaults of slander and hatred? What is most likely to disturb my peace? Why?

Your touch still has its ancient power. Touch me, Lord, into fellowship with Yourself till my whole being glows with Your peace and joy.KGD

When we are born again from above, quickened and raised up by God, we find it is possible to consider the lilies because we have not only the peace of God, but the very peace that characterized Jesus Christ. We are seated in heavenly places in Christ Jesus. The old way of doing things, the old fuss and fume are dead, and we are a new creation in Christ Jesus. In that new creation is manifested the very peace that was manifested in Jesus Christ.OBH

Reflection Questions

Do I fuss and fume over every inconvenience or do I consider the possibility that they were put there to slow me down and cause me to see something important that I would have missed?

When God raises us up into the heavenly places, He imparts to us the very purity of Jesus Christ. That is what the sanctified life means—the undisturbable range of His peace, the unshakeable, indefatigable power of His strength, and the unfathomable, crystalline purity of His holiness.OBH

Do you know how God speaks to His sons? He softly breathes His stern messages in the heavenly places. With what result? There is never any panic in His sons. The Son of God had pre-intimations of what was to happen. As we walk with the mind stayed where God places it by sanctification, in that way we will find that nothing strikes us with surprise or with panic. God never allows it to; He keeps us in perfect peace while He whispers His secrets and reveals His counsels. We are struck with panic whenever we turn out of the way.[OBH]

Reflection Questions

What admonition has God whispered to me? On what does He want me to focus so that nothing can cause me to panic? What does lack of peace tell me about my union with God?

When I have really transacted business with God on His covenant and have let go entirely, there is no sense of merit, no human ingredient in it at all, but a complete, overwhelming sense of having been brought into union with God, and the whole thing is transfigured with peace and joy.[OPG]

The thing that astonishes us when we get through to God is the way God holds us responsible for other lives. God holds us responsible for two things in connection with the lives He brings around us in the apparent haphazard of His providence—insistent waiting on God for them, and inspired instruction and warning from God to them. To enter into peace for ourselves without becoming either tolerantly un-watchful of other lives or an amateur providence over them, is supremely difficult.ᴼᴾᴳ

Reflection Questions

Am I behaving responsibly for the lives God has entrusted to me? Am I able to speak difficult truths in a calm and confident way?

The one thing Jesus Christ is after is the destruction of everything that would hinder the emancipation of men. The fact that people are happy and peaceful and prosperous is no sign that they are free from the sword of God. If their happiness and peace and well-being and complacency rests on an undelivered life, they will meet the sword before long, and all their peace and rest and joy will be destroyed.ᴾˢ

Which are the days that have furthered you most in the knowledge of God—the days of sunshine and peace and prosperity? Never! The days of adversity, the days of strain, the days of sudden surprises, the days when the earthly house of this tabernacle was strained to its last limit, those are the days when you learned the meaning of this passion of "Go." Any great calamity in the natural world—death, disease, bereavement— will awaken a man when nothing else would, and he is never the same again. We would never know the "treasures of darkness" if we were always in the place of placid security.PS

Reflection Questions

What does trouble teach me about peace?
Do I welcome God to interrupt my life or have I put a "Do Not Disturb" sign on the door of my life?

In spite of all our sense of uncleanness, in spite of all our rush and interest in the work of the world, and in spite of all our logic, the implicit sense of God will come and disturb our peace.PS

Children are sometimes afraid in the dark. Fear gets into their hearts and nerves and they get into a tremendous state; then they hear the voice of mother or father, and all is quietened and they go off to sleep. In our own spiritual experience it is the same. Some terror comes down the road to meet us and our hearts are seized with a tremendous fear; then we hear our own name called, and the voice of Jesus saying, "It is I, be not afraid," and the peace of God which passes understanding takes possession of our hearts.[SHL]

Reflection Questions

What frightens me? When am I most likely to be afraid? What words of Jesus alarm me? What words of Jesus take my fear away?

A man can never be the same again after having heard Jesus Christ preached. He may say he pays no attention to it; he may appear to have forgotten all about it, but he is never quite the same, and at any moment truths may spring up into his consciousness that will destroy all his peace and happiness.[RTR]

The natural man is not in distress, he is not conscious of conviction of sin, or of any disharmony. He is quite contented and at peace. Conviction of sin is the realization that my natural life is based on a disposition that will not have Jesus Christ. The Gospel does not present what the natural man wants but what he needs, and the Gospel awakens an intense resentment as well as an intense craving. We will take God's blessings and loving-kindnesses and prosperities, but when it comes to the need of having our disposition altered, there is opposition at once.[SHL]

Reflection Questions

What part of my disposition does God want to modify? Why do I resist? What assurance does He give me that peace comes only through conviction, confession, and conversion?

Never take an answer that satisfies your mind only; insist on an answer that satisfies by the "sound of gentle stillness." Jesus describes it as "My peace," the witness of God that goes all through you and produces a complete calm within.[PH]

The coming of Jesus Christ is not a peaceful thing, it is a disturbing, an overwhelming thing. Am I willing to be born into the realm Jesus Christ is in? If so, I must be prepared for chaos straight off in the realm I am in. The rule which has come in between God and man has to be eclipsed, and Jesus Christ's entering in means absolute chaos concerning the way I have been looking at things, a turning of everything upside down. The old order and the old peace must go, and we cannot get back peace on the old level.[SHL]

Reflection Questions

What chaos must I pass through to reach peace? What disturbance is required to overcome the old order? What false rule must be overthrown?

When Satan rules the hearts of natural men under the inspiration of the devil, they are not troubled, they are at peace, entrenched in clean worldliness (cf. Psalm 73), and before God can rule a man's kingdom He must first overthrow this false rule.[SHL]

189

Man himself is responsible for doing wrong things, and he does wrong things because of the wrong disposition that is in him. The true blame for sin lies in the wrong disposition, and the cunning of our nature makes us blame Satan when we should blame ourselves. When men go into external sins Satan is probably as much upset as the Holy Ghost, but for a different reason. Satan knows perfectly well that when men go into external sin and upset their lives, they will want another Ruler, a Saviour, a Deliverer; but as long as he can keep them in peace and unity and harmony apart from God he will do so.[SHL]

Reflection Questions

How well do I discern between peace from above and peace from below? How do I determine the difference?

Lord, today give me the intuitive, instinctive inspiration of Your Holy Spirit that I may discern You in all things. Fill the whole day with Your gracious presence and peace.[KGD]

Immediately the Spirit of God comes in we begin to realize what it means—everything that is not of God has to be cleaned out. People are surprised and say, "I asked for the Holy Spirit and expected that He would bring me joy and peace, but I have had a terrible time ever since." That is the sign He has come, He is turning out the "money-changers," that is, the things that make the temple into a trafficking place for self-realization.[SHL]

*R*eflection *Q*uestions

What disruption does Jesus cause in my life? What is He determined to clean out and throw out? What confidence do I place in diplomacy?

Be diplomatic. Be wise. Compromise in a shrewd way and you will get everything under your own control. That is the kind of thing the peace of the world is based on. We call it "diplomacy." Jesus maintained His faith in God's methods in spite of the temptations which were so wise from every standpoint except the standpoint of the Spirit of God.[SHL]

Socialism is immensely vague. It is the name for something which is all right in vision, but how are we going to establish the peace of the world so that nations will not go to war any more? God is longsuffering, and He is giving us ample opportunity to try whatever we like in both individual and national life. God is leaving us to prove that it cannot be done in any other than Jesus Christ's way, or the human race will not be satisfied.[SA]

Reflection Questions

What world systems have failed to usher in peace? In what way does Satan still rule in my life by assuring me that my ways and attitudes are right even though they conflict with the values and purpose of Christ?

When Satan rules, the souls of men are in peace. Before God can rule man's kingdom He must first overthrow this false rule. The coming of Jesus Christ is not a peaceful thing; it is overwhelming and frantically disturbing, because the first thing He does is to destroy every peace that is not based on a personal relationship to Himself.[SA]

In every period when the nations have been held in peace, it has been by an external authority, such as a Church, acting like an exotic, spreading its roots over the mass of humanity and holding it together. The Roman Catholic Church is a proof of this. There is only one thing as futile as the Roman Catholic Church and that is Protestantism. In Roman Catholicism the great dominating authority is Churchianity, the Church is vested with all authority. There are ways of bringing peace to a man's mind which are not true to the fundamental of things, and one of the most significant things during war is the change of mental front on the part of men as they face these things.[SA]

Reflection Questions

Am I willing to be born into the realm of Jesus? Am I prepared for temporary chaos in the way I look at life and the way I live?

Unto You, O Lord, I come, may Your beauty and grace and soothing peace be in and upon me this day, and may no wind or weather or anxiety ever touch Your peace in my life or in this place.[KGD]

It is a great thing to have our spiritual sight tested by the Celestial Optician, to watch the way in which He rectifies and readjusts our sight. There is one unmistakable witness that Jesus promised us, and that is the gift of His peace. No matter how complicated the circumstances may be, one moment of contact with Jesus and the fuss is gone, the panic is gone, all the shallow emptiness is gone, and His peace is put in, absolute tranquillity, because of what He says: "All power is given unto Me."

Reflection Questions

How has God tested and rectified my spiritual sight? What do I see more clearly now? How does clarity eliminate fuss and fear?

Oh, the fullness of peace and joy and gladness when we are persuaded that nothing "shall be able to separate us from the love of God, which is in Christ Jesus our Lord."[LG]

Just as Jesus Christ produces havoc in personal lives, so He will produce it all through on every line. For instance, if Jesus Christ had not obeyed the call of His Father, His own nation would not have blasphemed against the Holy Ghost. He ruined the career of a handful of fishermen, He disappointed and crushed the hopes of many and perturbed their peace. He continually produced havoc in people's lives.[SA]

Reflection Questions

Do I behave as if I believe that Jesus has all power on heaven and on earth? If not, why not? In what ways does the peace of Jesus keep me secure whether I am loved or hated?

What kind of peace had Jesus Christ? A peace that kept Him for thirty years at home with brothers and sisters who did not believe in Him; a peace that kept Him through three years of popularity, hatred, and scandal.[SA]

There are wonderful things about light, but there are terrible things also. When once the light of God's Spirit breaks into a heart and life that has been perfectly happy and peaceful without God, it is hell for that one. Light brings confusion and disaster. When light comes all the things of the night tremble. The night of heathenism is being split up, not by the incoming of civilization, but by the witness of men and women who are true to God.^{SSIY}

Reflection Questions

What has the light of the Lord revealed to me that is confusing, upsetting, or unclear? How does focusing on the Lord bring all that is blurry into a unified vision of peace and harmony?

Our Lord uses the eye as the symbol of conscience in a man who has been put right by the Holy Spirit. If we walk in the light as God is in the light, that will keep our eyes focused, and slowly and surely all our actions begin to be put into the right relationship, and everything becomes full of harmony and simplicity and peace.^{SSM}

Twenty centuries have passed since Jesus, the Prince of Peace, came and the angels proclaimed peace on earth. But where is peace?" The New Testament does not say that the angels prophesied peace: they proclaimed peace—peace to men of goodwill toward God. Jesus Christ came to manifest that God was with man, and by Him any man can be made a son of God according to the pattern of Jesus Christ. This is the Christian revelation.[PH]

Reflection Questions

Is my presence marked by Christ's peace? In what ways am I participating in the peace Christ proclaimed? In what ways am I preventing it from becoming a reality?

Those who are in The Way have a strong family likeness to Jesus, His peace marks them in an altogether conspicuous manner. The light of the morning is on their faces, and the joy of the endless life is in their hearts. Wherever they go, men are gladdened or healed, or made conscious of a need.[PH]

When a man comes to see what Jesus Christ demands, his peace of mind is upset. Are you so pure in heart that you never lust, never have a thought in the background of your mind that God could censure? If all Jesus Christ came to do was to put before us an ideal we cannot attain, we are happier without knowing it. But Jesus Christ did not come primarily to teach: He came to put within us His own disposition, that is, the Holy Spirit, whereby we can live a totally new life. A Christian is not consistent to hard and fast creeds, he is consistent only to the life of the Son of God in him.ᴾᴴ

Reflection Questions

Do I become agitated by God's unattainable standard of perfection or made calm and confident by the promise that the peace of Christ can accomplish the impossible?

Did Jesus Christ come for peace? He did; but it is a peace that is characteristic of Himself, not peace at any price. The peace that Jesus gives is never engineered by circumstances on the outside; it is a peace based on a personal relationship that holds through all tribulation.ᴾᴴ

To be "silent unto God" does not mean drifting into mere feeling, or sinking into reverie, but deliberately getting into the center of things and focusing on God. When you have been brought into relationship with God through the Atonement of the Lord Jesus Christ and are concentrating on Him, you will experience wonderful times of communion. As you wait only upon God, concentrating on the glorious outlines of His salvation, there will come into you the sleeping peace of God, the certainty that you are in the place where God is doing all in accordance with His will.[PH]

Reflection Questions

Have I entered the "sleeping peace" of God where I am at total rest because I know that God is working through me, I am not working for God?

The peace our Savior gives is the deepest thing a human personality can experience, it is almighty, a peace that passes all understanding.[PH]

No man can have his state of mind altered without suffering for it in his body, and that is why men do anything to avoid conviction of sin. When a worldly man who is happy, moral and upright, comes in contact with Jesus Christ, and that man must be persuaded that Jesus Christ has a better kind of life for him otherwise he feels he had better not have come across Him. If I am peaceful and happy and contented and living my life with my morality well within my own grasp, why does the Holy Spirit need to come in and upset the balance and make me miserable and unfit for anything? God's Book gives us the answer. Thousands of people are happy without God in this world, but that kind of happiness and peace is on a wrong level. Jesus Christ came to put us right with God that His own peace might reign.SHL

Reflection Questions

What mental and emotional contortions do I go through to avoid conviction of sin? How long am I able to maintain the twisted position of my own morality? Why do I resist being made right with God?

Salvation is always supernatural. The Holy Ghost brings me into union with God by dealing with that which broke the union. It is dangerous to preach a persuasive gospel, to try and persuade men to believe in Jesus Christ with the idea that if they do, He will develop them along the natural line. There is something to be destroyed first. Jesus Christ does not produce heaven and peace and delight straight off. He produces pain and misery and conviction and upset. But this is not all He came to do: He came to bring us into a supernatural union with His Father. When a man commits himself to Jesus Christ (belief is a moral act, not an intellectual act) then the Ascended Lord, by the Holy Ghost, brings the man into oneness with His Father. It is a supernatural union.[PR]

Reflection Questions

Is my sense of peace more like a truce between enemies or a permanent union and complete oneness with God through Christ? Why do I so often settle for the former?

Worrying is wicked in a Christian. How dare we be troubled if Almighty God Who made the world and everything in it is our Father? Why should we ignore God by worshipping what He has made, and then giving way to intellectual infidelity and doubting if He is wise and good? "Almighty God" means that there is no one or thing or force mightier. If you have ever been given the tiniest inkling of the meaning of what God said to Abraham, "I am God Almighty"—"El Shaddai," that moment will stand out in your experience infinitely more than any other experience. One moment's realization that Almighty God is your Father through Jesus Christ, and I defy anything to terrify you again for long. If we realize that nothing can happen without God's permission, we are kept in peace.[NJ]

Reflection Questions

What troubles me most? Do I believe my troubles are outside of God's control? Does it help to separate this familiar adjective into two words: All Mighty?

A closing thought to encourage those whose hearts are fainting in the way, those from whom the ideals of youth have fled, those to whom life holds no more promises: For years your life has been a boundless romance of possibilities; beckoning signs from lofty mountain peaks have lured the spirit on. But now the burden and the heat of the day have come, and the mountain tops are obscured in a dazing, dazzling heat, and the road is dusty and the mileage long, and the feet are weak and the endeavor is exhausting. Let me bring to you this message from Psalms as if it were a cup of water from the clear sparkling spring of life: "My help comes from the Lord Who made heaven and earth." He will take you up, He will re-make you, He will make your soul young and will restore to you the years that have been devoured, and place you higher than the loftiest mountain peak, safe in the arms of the Lord Himself, secure from all alarms, and with an imperturbable peace that the world cannot take away.[PH]

Index of Selections

206